# CATHOLIC PERSPECTIVES ON SPORTS

## From Medieval to Modern Times

### PATRICK KELLY, SJ

Paulist Press
New York / Mahwah, NJ

The scripture quotations contained herein are from the New Revised Standard Version: Catholic Edition Copyright © 1989 and 1993, by the Division of Christian Education of the National Council of the Churches of Christ in the United States of America. Used by permission. All rights reserved.

Passages from *The Institutes* of John Cassian, edited by Dennis McManus, translated by Boniface Ramsey, O.P. Copyright © 2000 by The Newman Press (Ancient Christian Writers Series). Used with permission of Paulist Press.

Passages from John of Damascus are taken from *On the Divine Images: Three Apologies against Those Who Attack the Divine Images* by John of Damascus, Copyright © 1980, St. Vladimir's Seminary Press. Used with Permission.

Passages from Irenaeus are taken from *Irenaeus of Lyons*, ed. Robert M. Grant, pp. 86, 87–88, 139–140, 167, 167–168, The Early Church Fathers Series (Routledge, 1997). Used with Permission.

*Chapter 2 Photo Credits*

The fourteenth-century stained-glass image of a "golfer" is from Gloucester Cathedral, England. Image by Richard Cann, used with permission of Gloucester Cathedral.

The fourteenth-century misericord with two ball players is from Gloucester Cathedral, England. Photo by the author. Used with permission of the author.

The fourteenth-century misericord with equestrian falconer is from Gloucester Cathedral, England. Photo by the author. Used with permission of the author.

The two images of ball players from a Franco-Flemish Book of Hours, circa 1300, are from the Walters Art Museum, Baltimore, MD. MS. W.88, fol. 59v and 70r. Used with permission of the Walters Art Museum, Baltimore, MD.

The image of blind man's bluff in a medieval garden is from the British Library, Stowe Ms. 955, f.7. Copyright © the British Library. Used with Permission.

Cover Image: courtesy of S. Pytel / Shutterstock.com
Cover design by Sharyn Banks
Book design by Lynn Else

Copyright © 2012 by Patrick Kelly, SJ

Library of Congress Control Number: 2012028255
ISBN 978-0-8091-4795-3

Published by Paulist Press
997 Macarthur Boulevard
Mahwah, New Jersey 07430

www.paulistpress.com

Printed and bound in the United States of America

No honest game is entirely lacking in the capacity to instruct. I think that this delightful exercise with the ball represents a significant philosophy for us.

Cardinal Nicholas of Cusa,
*The Game of Spheres*, 1463

To Mike,
Go Irish! Blessings in the year.
Fr Pat SJ

# CONTENTS

For you, Mom and Dad
My first teachers in the Catholic faith

# ILLUSTRATIONS

# ACKNOWLEDGMENTS

In some ways I feel like the whole of my life has contributed to this book. This is because I have enjoyed playing sports from the time I was very young. In this sense, it is not possible to thank everyone who has played a role in helping this book come to fruition. But it is true that I owe a great deal to my coaches and teammates from grade school through college. The important formational experiences I had during those years convinced me that play and sport were, indeed, humanly significant. And my coaches and teammates played an important role in helping to shape those experiences.

I began working on parts of this project while in doctoral studies at Claremont Graduate University. I thank, in particular, Louis Ruprecht, the chair of my dissertation committee for his encouragement and wise counsel. Anselm Min also asked many probing questions that made me think more deeply about the project. Mihaly Csikszentmihalyi, in particular, has been an inspiration to me. He is an enormously creative social scientist who is also very accessible to his students. I have appreciated his encouragement and the enjoyable and fruitful time I have spent with him and his wife Isabella over the years. Ann Taves was a great mentor when I was her teaching assistant and has been very supportive of my interest in this area of research.

John W. O'Malley, SJ, has had a great influence on my development as a scholar. He read the first two chapters of this book; I thank him for his historian's attention to detail and his encouragement. Thanks also to Mick McCarthy, SJ, who read the third chapter and provided advice. And to Dan Dombrowski, for reading several chapters and providing helpful feedback. A special thank you to Stephen Sundborg, SJ, who read the entire manuscript and provided insightful comments and suggestions, many of which I have incorporated into the book. Of course, I am solely responsible for the final form this book has taken.

I thank Catherine Smith, who has been an invaluable help with the early editing of the manuscript and a source of encouragement throughout.

The initial feedback that Mark-David Janus, CPS, president and publisher of Paulist Press, provided to me regarding the manuscript was immensely helpful. I benefited from our few conversations very much. Many thanks to my editor, Jim Quigley, for his ability to see problems with the writing and to come up with ingenious ways to solve them.

I have used this text in some of my classes about sport and religion at Seattle University, and I thank my students for their questions and comments about the material. My colleagues in the Theology and Religious Studies Department have also always been very supportive of my work in the area of sport, for which I am grateful. I did a great deal of work on this project during a one-quarter release from teaching provided to junior faculty at Seattle University; I thank Dean David Powers and Provost Isiaah Crawford for this release.

I have lived in the Arrupe Jesuit Residence at Seattle University during many of the years I was working on this book. I thank the Jesuits in this community for their support. They are an unusually good group of men and Jesuits. A special thanks to the "Pats" in the community.

## Acknowledgments

Finally, I thank my brothers and sisters, Dan, Nancy, Sharon, and Sean, and their spouses and families. I have always valued your support over the years and hope you have felt supported by me. A special thanks to my mom and dad, to whom this book is dedicated.

# INTRODUCTION

In the past twenty-five years or so, historians, sociologists, theologians, and religious studies scholars have written a great deal about the influence that Protestant Christians have had on modern sport in England and the United States. More recently, theologians and religious studies scholars have been debating and discussing whether sport can be understood as a "civil" or "folk" religion in the United States. This research seems to offer a different perspective on modern sport from that of Allen Guttmann, who argued in his book *From Ritual to Record: The Nature of Modern Sports* that one of the distinguishing features of modern sport was its secular character.

Very little research has been done, however, on the relationship between Catholic theological and spiritual traditions and sport in the West. This omission is curious, especially given the importance of the Catholic faith during the medieval and early modern periods in Europe. When historians and other scholars write about sport during these periods, they tend to describe the games and sports themselves and simply bracket the religious dimension entirely, or they argue that these practices took place for the most part in spite of the Catholic faith of the people, a faith that taught them to regard the body as evil, pleasure as the gateway to sin, and so on. What is lacking is any positive account of the relationship between Catholic theological and spiritual traditions and the games and sports of these periods. This is part of what I provide in this book.

1

During the medieval period, Catholics participated in games and sports on feast days and Sundays and depicted such activities in prayer books and on woodcuts and stained glass windows in churches and cathedrals. Catholic humanists during the Renaissance included time for play and sport in the first schools that educated primarily lay people and the Jesuits followed their lead in subsequent centuries. The inclusion of games and sports in the Jesuits' schools would be especially important, as they were operating some eight hundred schools by the mid-eighteenth century in Europe and other parts of the world.

The ease with which games and sports were incorporated into medieval and early modern Catholic cultures and educational institutions was supported by several factors, including the Christian understanding of the material world as good and of the human person as a unity of body and soul (or body, soul, and spirit); the view that a virtuous person should be moderate in his studies or work and take time to engage in play and recreation; and an understanding of the relationship between faith and culture, which tended toward the acceptance of non-Christian customs and cultural traditions that were good in themselves (or at least not objectionable on moral grounds), and their inclusion in the religious tradition. For some theologians, such as Thomas Aquinas and Nicholas of Cusa, play itself was even understood to have spiritual significance.

Catholics brought these cultural and theological traditions with them to the United States, where they engaged in play and sport routinely and without anxiety and incorporated them in their schools as a matter of course. This approach was very different from that of the Protestant majority in the United States and was a part of what made lay Catholics seem alien and unusual to the Protestant majority when Catholics first arrived in large numbers in the nineteenth century.

Research on Catholic influences in earlier periods helps us

to better understand sport during those periods. It also brings into clear relief times when important changes happened that have made it difficult to develop a theology or spirituality of sport in the contemporary context. In particular, the longer history of sport helps us to see the importance of the emergence of the Puritans and the work ethic in the sixteenth century. In large part because the Puritans associated godliness with one's calling or work, they regarded play with a new level of suspicion and regularly associated it with sin. Another important change occurred when the emphasis shifted from the unity of the human person, body and soul, to a dualism of body and soul. The seventeenth-century philosopher Rene Descartes played an important role in this process. Prior to Descartes, the tendency was to *distinguish* between the body and soul, but within a broader emphasis on the unity of the human person. Descartes described the body and soul as polar opposites: the body as material, extended, and unthinking, and the soul as immaterial, unextended, and thinking. His successors were left with the seemingly impossible task of figuring out how body and soul, described in this way, interacted.

Both the Puritan emphasis on work and suspicion of play and the Cartesian dualism of body and soul undercut the foundation upon which a theology or spirituality of sport could have been developed in the modern period. After all, if play is primarily thought of as associated with sin, one would hardly think of looking at human experiences of play to learn anything about the human person or the Christian life. Also, if what happens in the body is not related in any meaningful way to consciousness (to say nothing of the "spirit"), then what is the point of taking seriously bodily activities such as play and sport from a theological or spiritual perspective?

The Catholic Church was changing a great deal as we moved into the modern world, which also made it difficult to develop a theology or spirituality of sport in the contemporary context. In the face of the challenges posed by the Protestant reformers, Catholic theologians spent a great deal of their time offering systematic answers to issues having to do with papal supremacy, the number and nature of the sacraments, the relationship between faith and works, and so on. The increasing acceptance of the scientific mode of knowing, the Enlightenment, and political revolutions all posed new challenges to theologians and church leaders as well, who began to see themselves as "at war" with the modern world. Theologians and church leaders complained about the focus of the modern world on material things, including the body. In his first speech that touched on sport in 1940, for example, Pope Pius XII told young men of Catholic Action that even though people in the modern world were fascinated by physical exercises and sport, the church is "a mother who will teach you more the things of the mind and the spirit than those of the body and the material order."[1] In general, the antagonism between the church and the modern world meant that theologians and church leaders were not paying attention to cultural developments, including those taking place in the realm of sport.

The resources from the earlier theological and spiritual traditions provide a rationale for Catholic theologians to begin reflecting on sport as an aspect of culture in the contemporary context. In particular, the emphasis of theologians that the human person is a unity of body and soul (or body, soul, and spirit) makes it important to pay attention to bodily activities such as sport, which necessarily affect consciousness and spirit. The way theologians understood the relationship between faith and culture is also part of the rationale for theologians to reflect on sport in the contemporary context. St. Paul, the apostle to the Gentiles, was one of the more important figures in the tradition in this regard. He was a Greek-speaking Jew, who after his dramatic conversion spent the rest of his life making the gospel known to the Greek-speaking world. He did so by entering into a dialogue with the Greeks based on their own cultural and intellectual heritage, which included their athletic contests. St. Paul's approach had a significant influence on Christians in future generations. Pope John Paul II drew on St. Paul's approach in encouraging Catholics in our own context to pay attention to sport and regard it with respect and esteem. John Paul II also emphasized the importance of working to correct and elevate sport, so that it serves the human person and his or her integral development, including in the area of spirituality.

The earlier theological and spiritual traditions also have much to offer to the discussion of contemporary problems in sport. In particular, the earlier emphasis on moderation as central to a life of virtue has much relevance. For Thomas Aquinas, the humanists, and early Jesuits, a person should not be studying or working all the time. Such a life would be immoderate. This is why they argued that play and recreation were an important part of life. Indeed, for Thomas Aquinas, *it was possible to sin by having too little play in one's life.* This understanding of virtue is important in our own context in the United States, where the play element is disappearing from sport in general in our own time, and even from youth sport, which is rapidly becoming overserious and worklike.

Moderation with respect to study and work is also important for college and elite-level athletes. These athletes are encouraged to work hard and excel in all areas of their lives, but they often have difficulty knowing how to relax and recreate when they are not playing their sport. The personal problems that these athletes have off the court or playing field are often brought on because they have not yet found ways to "rest and recreate their souls" that are healthy and restorative. The importance of moderating one's desires is relevant in a broader sense, as well. It is a lack of moderation with respect to the desire to win, for example, that has led to scandals around the use of performance-enhancing drugs and recurring violations of National Collegiate Athletic Association (NCAA) rules in intercollegiate athletics.

Traditionally, prominent Catholic theologians have emphasized the similarities between play and Christian spirituality. In light of this heritage, Catholic theologians should be protecting and safeguarding the play element in sport, and particularly in youth sport. After all, if similarities exist between play and spirituality, then the play element of sport would be a rich area to explore to discover the spiritual significance of sport participation. Earlier I mentioned the Puritans, who, because of their emphasis on the connection between godliness and one's calling or work, tended to regard play with suspicion and associated it with sin. But not all Protestants in the United States followed the Puritans in this regard. Indeed, some Protestant theologians both historically and in our own context have lamented the overemphasis on industriousness and the loss of the play element in American culture. This dissident wing within Protestant theology has been concerned to articulate the spiritual significance of play. There is considerable room, then, for ecumenical research and writing in this area. Scholars in disciplines such as philosophy, anthropology, and psychology have also done a great deal of research and writing on the play element in sport. Catholic theologians should be in dialogue with this research as well, so as to be able to articulate the human and spiritual significance of play in a way that corresponds with what is known to be true about the human person in light of contemporary scholarship.

June 15, 2012
Feast of the Sacred Heart

# CHAPTER ONE

# "NO PURITAN PALL HOVERED OVER SUNDAYS"

No theological principle or focus is more characteristic of Catholicism or more central to its identity
than the principle of sacramentality. The Catholic
vision sees God in and through all things: other
people, communities, movements, events, places,
objects, the world at large, the whole cosmos.[1]

Most Catholic theologians would agree with Richard
McBrien's assertion that no principle or focus is more
characteristic of Catholicism than the principle of
sacramentality, which emphasizes God's presence in creation
and in various aspects of culture and the importance of finding
"God in all things." It is curious, then, that Catholic theologians
have had so little to say about sport, which has always been
present in all cultures of the world (in one form or another)
and, since the beginning of the twentieth century, has been
more pervasive than ever before. The lack of reflection by
Catholic theologians in the United States is even more puz-
zling, given the significance sport has had and continues to
have in the American context. Sociologist George Sage points
out that sport is so pervasive in the United States that to
ignore it is to overlook one of the most important aspects of
American society. He comments that sport is a social phenomenon that extends into such areas of life as education, politics,

economics, art, the mass media, and even international diplomatic relations. The significance that sport has in the United States has led some commentators to suggest that "if there is a religion in America today, it is sport."[2]

Children start participating in sport when they are very young. In the United States today, many begin playing baseball, football, and basketball in organized leagues at six years of age or younger and then advance through different levels of play. They start playing organized soccer and hockey at even younger ages. In the past thirty years or so in the United States, children have begun to specialize in one sport earlier than ever before, in the hope that they can get a head start on their peers in the competition for a college scholarship or a professional contract. It would be difficult to overestimate the impact of this participation on the human formation of the young people involved.

And yet, Catholic theologians, particularly in the United States, have been virtually silent on the topic of sport. Why is this the case?

The most common answer given to this question assumes that there is something fundamental to Christianity that is antithetical to sport. This "something" has to do with Christian attitudes toward the body. Indeed, a recurring narrative in the writing of the history of sport tells how Christians up until the time of the Reformation placed great emphasis on the soul and the spiritual realm and disregarded, if not disdained, the body. For some scholars, this was the reason that little importance was given to games and sport during the medieval and early modern periods. In these accounts it was only after the repressive regime of the Puritans in England and America that more enlightened views about the body began to take hold. In the nineteenth century, games and sports began to be accepted by reasonable people and to have a more prominent place in society. The suggestion is that Christians and theologians have only recently, and somewhat reluctantly, embraced sports.[3]

Is there some validity to this analysis? It is true, after all, that some writers in the early church, among them Tertullian, were hostile to "spectacles." In about 393 CE, thirteen years after the Roman Empire officially became Christian, the Olympic games were ended, not to be revived until the late nineteenth century. It was common for early and medieval theologians, many of whom were writing in monastic settings removed from the world, to emphasize the relative importance of the soul over the body. This relative valuation of soul over body influenced later reflections on the relationship between the church and the world and clerical and lay members of the church. Isn't it true that some of these traditions led to the perception that play was associated with the loosening of constraints and would surely lead to sin, and that "spirituality" was associated with settings removed from the world and had to do with the soul more than the body? Perhaps it is possible to answer yes to this question.

And yet, these were not the only traditions influencing early and medieval Christianity. One of the earliest doctrinal controversies in the church had to do with the Gnostic teaching that the material world and the human body were not capable of participating in the spiritual life. This teaching was opposed by the second-century theologian Irenaeus and other early Christian theologians, who emphasized that God created all things on earth and in heaven, corporeal and incorporeal—and pronounced all things good. The human body, for these authors, was constitutive of human personhood. Thus, for Irenaeus it was appropriate that Christians "hope for the...salvation of the whole person, that is, of soul and body."[4]

Similar controversies continued to show up in the life of the church with subsequent groups such as the Manicheans, the Cathars, and Waldensians. These groups also taught a dualism that viewed the material world and the human body as associated with evil and hence as incompatible with the spiritual life. Important theologians such as Augustine and Thomas Aquinas, among others, rejected such an understanding of the Christian life, insisting rather on the goodness of the material world and on a conception of the human person as a unity of body and soul or body, soul, and spirit. Their arguments were intimately related to basic Christian beliefs regarding the goodness of the created world, the Word becoming flesh (the incarnation) and the resurrection of the whole person, body and soul.

If Christians understood the material world to be good and the person to be a unity of body and soul, then it made sense that Christian religious practices would take the material world and the human body seriously. And they did. Indeed, the earliest Christians were already following Jesus's example and celebrating the Eucharist before most of the books that were to make up the New Testament were written (notice that the apostle Paul is writing his letters to established churches that were already celebrating the Eucharist). Paul would be the first person to develop a theology of the sacraments, though, and early theologians such as Irenaeus elaborated on his writings.

Irenaeus emphasized the coherence among the various Christian doctrines. As already noted, in his view a central problem with Gnostic theology was its belief that the human body, being a part of the material world, was not capable of participating in the spiritual life. This view showed up in many Gnostic teachings, including their denial of the resurrection of the body. Irenaeus appeals to Christian belief and practice in relation to the Eucharist and asks how one can "deny that the flesh is receptive of the gift of God, which is eternal life, when it has been nourished by the body and blood of the Lord and is a member of him?"[5] Indeed, for Irenaeus, the Eucharist proclaims

> fittingly the communion and unity of the flesh and the spirit. For as the bread, which is produced from the earth, when it receives the invocation of God is no longer common bread, but the eucharist, consisting of two realities, the earthly and the heavenly, so also our bodies, when they receive the eucharist, are no longer corruptible, but have the hope of resurrection.[6]

When the sacraments were challenged in the thirteenth century by the Cathars and Waldensians, the same question about the relationship between the material and spiritual world was at issue. As Thomas Aquinas put it at the time:

> That one might not believe visible things evil of their nature…it was fitting that through the visible things themselves the remedies of salvation be applied to human beings. Consequently, it would appear that visible things are good of their nature—as created by God….Thus, of course, one excludes the error of certain heretics who want every visible thing of this kind removed from the sacraments of the church.[7]

It is also instructive that one of the central controversies in the history of Christian spirituality hinged on the issue of the relationship between the material and the spiritual world. This was the controversy around the appropriateness of the use of images in Christian worship. When this controversy reached a point of crisis in the eighth century, John of Damascus argued for the appropriateness of the use of images by pointing to the traditional Christian liturgical practices that were intimately linked to the material world and performed with bodily gestures. He suggests to his opponents that if they want to get rid of images, they should get rid of all of these practices as well.

> If you say that only intellectual worship is worthy of God, then take away all corporeal things: light, the fragrance of incense, prayer made with the voice. Do away with the divine mysteries which are fulfilled through matter: bread, wine, the oil of chrism, the sign of the cross. All these things are matter! Take away the cross and the sponge of the crucifixion, and the spear which pierced His life-giving side. Either give up honoring all these things, or do not refuse to honor images. Matter is filled with divine grace through prayer addressed to those portrayed in images.[8]

Medieval religious drama, one artistic genre in which the central mysteries of the Christian faith were "played" out through the liturgical year, could only have become such an important aspect of medieval cultures if the arguments of theologians, such as St. John, regarding the appropriateness of the use of images were persuasive. But care needs to be taken not to overstate the role that theologians played in this area. The theologians debated the topic to begin with because people—including especially those who were unable to read—were already using images in their devotional practices. In the case of the plays, it was lay people who took the lead in staging and acting in these; the various guilds of laborers were responsible for putting on the plays on the different feast days and holy days. Later, dramas dealing with religious and nonreligious themes were staged by students in the humanist and early Jesuit schools. People from every segment of European society attended these plays.

One of the curious features about the writing of the history of Christian spirituality is that lay Catholics tend to be left out of the picture. If one takes the time to simply take a look at *what lay Catholics were doing* in the medieval period, one notices that they went on pilgrimages to sites with the relics of saints; participated in processions; prayed in churches and cathedrals with stained glass windows and woodcuts; put on mystery and morality plays; sculpted—and venerated—statues; painted scenes from the Bible; fingered their rosary beads; lit candles; crawled to the cross; put ashes on their forehead; engaged in corporal works of mercy and participated in the sacraments that made use of bread, wine, oil, fire, water, and so on. In other words, they engaged in a whole variety of bodily activities, which they believed (and the theologians, priests, and bishops gathered at church councils concurred with them) were also spiritual.

Lay people also participated in games and sports of various kinds on Sundays and on the feast days of the church year. As William Baker writes in the book *Sports in the Western World*:

> No puritan pall hovered over Sundays. After the sermon and the sacraments in the morning, villagers lounged or played on Sunday afternoon. For youths, especially, re-creation meant recreation. Nor was recreation confined to Sunday afternoons. The church calendar of holidays, aligned with ancient seasonal patterns, granted festive occasions at Easter, during harvest season, and at Christmas. Throughout Europe this basic pattern was followed....Blessed by church leaders, accepted by landlords, and sanctified by tradition, some of these seasonal breaks in labor ran for several days. Wine or ale, music, and dance accompanied the peasant games and frolic.[9]

It is significant that the feast days were so numerous that they typically accounted for around one-third of the calendar year.

When the humanists began running the first schools primarily for lay students in the late fourteenth century, they included time for the students to play games and sports in the daily schedule. They were influenced in this regard by the medieval traditions just mentioned and also by what the classical Greek and Latin authors had to say about the importance of the body and sports in the educational process. The early Jesuits followed the humanist lead and incorporated time and space for games and sports in the first schools they opened in the late sixteenth century—and in all of their subsequent schools. This development would have a significant influence on education in the Western world because of the sheer number of Jesuit schools. They were running nearly eight hundred schools in Europe and in other parts of the world by the mid-eighteenth century.

# SPORT, CULTURES, AND CHRISTIANITY IN EARLY MODERN AND MODERN PERIODS

## *The Reformation and the Puritans*

Much of what has been described previously concerning religious attitudes and practices came under heavy criticism during the Reformation in England and in the colonies of the New World. Henry VIII began by reducing the number of feast days and holy days in the calendar. This development significantly reduced the time for games and sport during any given year. Henry's disputes with Rome, however, had to do with his wish for an annulment to secure a male heir and were not primarily theological in nature. He eventually defended many of the traditional Catholic practices against those whom he regarded as overzealous reformers. The reigns of Edward and, in particular, Elizabeth would bring about more far-reaching reforms with regard to the use of images in worship and the sacraments, as well as the devotional practices that had grown up around the saints and Mary.

The Puritans took matters even further, however. Following in the tradition of John Calvin, but accentuating some of his main themes, they emphasized the radical sinfulness of the human person before God (that is, his total corruption and depravity). This view left them suspicious of what was merely human and not found in God's word. Feast days and holy days fell into this category, as did the play and games that took place on them. As John Northbrooke wrote in 1577:

> And where you say that holydayes (as they are termed), were invented in old time for pastimes, I think you say truth. For ye Pope appointed them (and not God in his word), and that only to traine up the people in ignorance and ydleness, whereby halfe of the year, and more, was overpassed (by their idyle holydayes) in loitering and vaine pastimes, &c., in restraining men from their handy labors and occupations.[10]

The reference to "labors" and "occupations" in the last sentence is crucial. With the Puritans, *godliness* becomes linked to *work* in a new way in the history of Christian spirituality. This emphasis had its roots in the writings of Martin Luther and John Calvin about the importance of the "calling" in the life of every Christian. Luther and Calvin were not quite as rigorous in their theology as the Puritans would be, however, and so were more understanding about the need for recreation and games. With the Puritans, there was more anxiety about relaxing the tension associated with one's godly calling. This is one of the reasons why they regarded play with such suspicion and started to associate it routinely with sin.

A story recounted by Governor William Bradford about a confrontation he had with newly arrived settlers in Plymouth colony on Christmas Day in 1621 is a good example of the new Puritan emphasis on work and the suspicion of play. In good Puritan fashion, Bradford had no use for the celebration of feast days and holy days, including Christmas. He was particularly concerned about people being kept from their work by playing stool-ball and other such games on Christmas Day. He comments, referring to himself in the third person:

> On the day called Christmasday, the Governor called them out to work as was used. But the most of this new company excused themselves and said it went against their consciences to work on that day. So the Governor told them that if they made it matter of conscience, he would spare them till they were better informed; so he led away the rest and left them. But when they came home at noon from their work, he found them in the street at play, openly; some pitching the bar, and some at stool-ball and such like sports. So he went to them and took away their implements and told them that was against his conscience, that they should play and others work. If they made the keeping of it a matter of devotion, let them keep (it in) their houses; but there should be no gaming or reveling in the streets. Since which time nothing has been attempted that way, at least openly.[11]

According to William Baker, Bradford's "stern stance was directed as much against the recognition of Christmas, that old pagan, Catholic holiday, as against mere play."[12]

These kinds of sensibilities would have a profound influence on the structure of social life in the early colonies. Nearly all of the traditional European feast days and holy days were eliminated from the calendar. As a new six-day workweek emerged, Sunday became *the* day of religious significance. The central controversies revolved around what it was licit to do on Sundays. And whether it was acceptable to play games or not was central to this debate. Both magistrates and ministers decided it was not and enacted laws to this effect. The changes went far beyond Sundays, however. Games and physical exercises did not have a significant place in the daily lives of the students at Harvard or the other colleges in the early years of their existence.[13] And no dramas were performed, religious or otherwise, for nearly two centuries.

Such developments led to a situation in the United States in the nineteenth century in which work had seemingly taken over all aspects of life and play seemed to be missing. The geologist Sir Charles Lyell, visiting from England in 1846, commented on this phenomenon. From the time he and his fellow travelers landed in New England, he wrote, "We seemed to have been in a country where all, whether rich or poor, were labouring from morning till night, without ever indulging in a holiday. I had sometimes thought that the national motto should be, 'All work and no play.'"[14]

Some influential Protestant theologians also lamented the loss of the play element in American culture. In 1855, Edward Everett Hale, a Unitarian clergyman, pointed out in his sermon "Public Amusement for Poor and Rich" that even the holidays Americans did have lacked a playful and exuberant spirit:

> You see, every year, throngs of people who have come into town to spend "Independence Day", sadly pacing hand in hand up the streets and down again, unamused, unrejoicing,—wishing that the holiday were over, before it has half gone by. I have wished that

> some man of intellectual power as severe as Goethe's
> …would appear, to shew our hard-workers how to rest
> themselves—our hard-thinkers how to play. That man
> has never come, and those workers do not know how.[15]

Many of the characteristics of modern sport as we know it were developing in the late nineteenth century. Some commentators see the development of modern sport as something of a reaction to the body- and soul-numbing nature of life in the factories during this time. These commentators point out that sport provided a release from the harsh demands of work in the factories and allowed people an opportunity for bodily expression and exuberance on their own terms. But, as they developed, the games and sports also began to take on characteristics of life in the factories, such as a mechanized view of the body and concern for efficiency, as well as a detailed and methodical approach to management. In the early twentieth century, when it became apparent that sport itself was a saleable commodity, businessmen were quick to take notice, and the relationship between sport and business concerns was soon prospering. Some commentators suggest that our games and sport could finally have a place in American culture only when they became intimately linked to work and the business world that *were* highly valued and understood to be related to spiritual values.

The problem with such a development is that it allows for a continuation of our Puritan heritage, which sees little or no value in the activities themselves. In such a context, those who are interested in theology or spirituality have tended not to look at the games and sports themselves to learn anything about the human person or the Christian life. Ironically, such an approach allows the games and sports to become even more susceptible to being viewed solely in instrumental terms, as mere commodities. There is a relationship between this dynamic and persons participating in sport viewing themselves as having instrumental value in terms of whether they are successful or not, which continues to be a problem for participants in sport at all ages and levels in our own context.

## Early Modern and Modern Catholicism

The Catholic Church was changing as we entered the modern world, and some of the changes have their roots in the late sixteenth century. The bishops who gathered at the Council of Trent had responded to many of the challenges of the Reformation theologians and also established an impressive disciplinary system that was meant to keep bishops (yes, they were disciplining themselves!) in their dioceses, along with higher standards for seminaries to ensure that priests were educated and didn't depart from church doctrine. Catechisms were written, some for lay people and others for children. Many clerics began to expend more energy rooting out "pagan" elements of popular religious observance. Clerics and theologians also emphasized in a new way the importance of "purity" in one's moral life, and especially in the area of sexuality. Because basic doctrines of the church were being questioned by the reformers and their successors, Catholic theologians spent much of their energy after the Council of Trent developing clear and distinct answers to questions related to topics such as the authority of the pope, the validity of the sacraments and religious life, how the process of justification occurs, and so on.

The challenges to the Catholic Church did not stop with the Reformation, however. The increased acceptance of science and its methods of inquiry and the rise of Enlightenment sensibilities also posed challenges to theologians who wanted to go on with business as usual. Bernard Lonergan points out that theologians responded to these challenges by introducing the new branch of theology known as "dogmatic theology." "When modern science began, when the Enlightenment began," Lonergan writes, "then the theologians began to reassure one another about their certainties."[16] They did so by offering invincible proof of their positions, which they deduced from clear and distinct premises of faith and reason.

As we have seen, Christians in the early and medieval periods insisted on the unity of the human person, body and soul. This sensibility can be seen in their religious practices, which take seriously both the material world and the human body. In the early part of the seventeenth century, beginning with Descartes, there was a new emphasis on the contrast between the body and soul, however. According to Descartes, the body is material, extended in space, and unthinking, and the soul is immaterial, unextended, and thinking. Because he described body and soul as polar opposites in this way, it was very difficult for him and subsequent philosophers to understand how the two interacted. There also emerges with Descartes a new valuing of "disengaged reason." According to Descartes, the first step in arriving at knowledge was to distance oneself from the body, custom, and tradition. One should only affirm what could be known clearly and distinctly, independently of such sources.

According to Charles Taylor, one of the most significant developments associated with the elite-led religious reform movements, and with the thought of Descartes, was that bodily engagement with the world was no longer regarded as the avenue to truth or to spiritual experience as it had been in earlier periods. Taylor refers to this development as "excarnation," by which he means "the steady disembodying of spiritual life, so that it is less and less carried in deeply meaningful bodily forms, and lies more and more 'in the head.'"[17]

This process of "excarnation," or disembodying of the spiritual life and its movement "into the head," had an impact on Catholic theologians and church leaders. It is very evident in a talk Pope Pius XII gave to the young men of Catholic Action in 1940, one of the first statements of the popes that dealt with sport. In this talk, the pope told the young men:

> Everything which has to do with physical exercise, with contests, rivalry, sport, interests and attracts the youth of today. But young Christians know that intellectual exercises and especially the race toward intellectual light...are all the more beautiful, noble, and gripping as knowledge and strength of the mind surpass and outstrip muscular strength and the precarious agility and suppleness of the body's members.[18]

Pius XII regards the fascination of people with physical exercise and sport as an instance of a broader modern preoccupation with the material world that tends to neglect spiritual values. By way of contrast, he emphasizes that Christians should value "intellectual exercises" and the "race toward intellectual light." The problem is that his statement makes it sound like the spiritual life is not associated with bodily activities such as sport but rather takes place "in the head." This view is expressed in starker terms later in his talk to the young men of Catholic Action, when he said:

> You are seeking a mother who will teach you more the things of the mind and the spirit than those of the body and the material order. And where have you found that mother and that most loving teacher? Where did she communicate to you, not the life of the

body, but the life of the spirit, the most high destiny of your soul?[19]

Another important event that profoundly shaped the attitude of the Catholic Church toward the modern world was the French Revolution. It is significant that the French Revolution, in contrast to the American, was antireligious and anticlerical at its core.[20] While the ideals of the French Revolution were "liberty, equality and fraternity," Catholics, and the institutional church in particular, suffered very badly during this period. The powers of the papacy over the church in France were severely curtailed. If you were a priest and your parish was turned into a Temple of Reason, or if you were a monk or a nun and your monastery was taken over by the government, you probably would not have viewed this as a time of great liberty, equality, or fraternity. The effect of these developments on the hierarchy of the church and many of its theologians was to move them into a defensive and reactionary stance toward all of the ideas and developments associated with the revolution in France. Such a stance is expressed in a dramatic way in papal documents from the nineteenth and early twentieth centuries, such as the Syllabus of Errors and the condemnations of Americanism and of modernism.[21]

The American Revolution and the Enlightenment sensibilities that accompanied it, on the other hand, were intertwined with Protestant theological and spiritual traditions, and most Americans (and the vast majority of the citizens in the early colonies were Protestant) did not feel a need to choose between their revolutionary and faith commitments. Rather, there was something of a symbiotic relationship between the two. But these Protestant roots of American culture meant that Catholics tended to be regarded with a good deal of suspicion by the Protestant majority, as enemies of the kind of freedom associated with Reformation spiritual traditions, the Enlightenment emphasis on thinking for oneself, and democratic political traditions. This was one of the reasons why Catholics, when they began arriving in the United States in large numbers in the middle of the nineteenth century, were often greeted with little enthusiasm and at times with hostility.

The Catholic Church in the United States became more organized and institutionalized in the late nineteenth century than it had been in earlier periods. Bishops who received their training in Rome began to be appointed to dioceses around the country and to emphasize uniformity in belief and practice in a new way. This was especially the case after the papal condemnations of Americanism and modernism. In part, due to the lack of acceptance by the mainstream culture, there was a tendency for Catholics to try to set up a "separate society" wherein all aspects of life would be taken care of by the institutional church. This meant, in the view of church leadership, that ordinary Catholics would not need to engage the surrounding culture and so could be kept free from its less than desirable influences. The establishment of a Catholic school system was an important part of this process.

In Catholic schools, however, sports were a part of the daily lives of the students, and eventually high schools and universities fielded teams that represented the schools. Sports contests with public school teams became one important point of contact with the surrounding culture for lay Catholics beginning in the late nineteenth and early twentieth centuries. And many Catholics viewed these sporting contests as an opportunity to show that they were as capable (that is, as strong, smart, resourceful, and so on) as the Protestants and to claim a place for themselves in the wider society. This was done successfully at many Catholic high schools around the country and at institutions of higher education such as the University of Notre Dame in Indiana and Immaculata College in Philadelphia, which had one of the country's earliest, and most successful, women's basketball teams.[22]

There was very little, if any, reflection on what these sports contests were all about, however, or how they were related to Catholic beliefs or values. Theologians and spiritual writers were certainly quiet on the subject. The view of church leadership seemed to be that as long as Catholics were living their lives within the confines of the institutional church, one could be sure that everything was in its proper place and that all was right with the world. When it came to sports, however, the walls of the institution were probably more porous than they had thought.

If Catholic theologians were so quiet about the sports that were pervasive within Catholic educational institutions, it is not surprising that they had nothing to say about sports as they became professionalized either, even though many lay Catholics were playing professional sports and, indeed, were some of the more prominent figures involved in sports at the highest levels.

# CONCLUSION

A recurring narrative in the writing of the history of sport in the West assumes that Christians prior to the Reformation placed a great emphasis on the soul and the spiritual realm and disregarded, if not disdained, the body. According to some scholars, this is why Christians did not pay attention to or encourage sports during the medieval period. This assumption about Christian attitudes toward the body prior to the Reformation is not accurate, however. Rather, Christians in the early and medieval periods insisted repeatedly on the importance of the material world and that the person was a unity of body and soul (or body, soul, and spirit). Such emphases provided the rationale for the emergence of religious practices, such as the sacraments and the use of images in worship, in which the body was integrally involved, and led to the emergence of religious drama. These emphases were also a part of what led Christians to be comfortable with bodily activities such as play and sport.

During the medieval period, Christians played games and sports on Sundays and the feast days and holy days. Starting in the late fourteenth century, games and sports were included in the curriculum of the humanist schools, and the Jesuits followed their lead in subsequent centuries. The Jesuits, in particular, would play an important role in Western education in this regard, because of their vast network of schools.

The reformers rejected many of the religious sensibilities and practices of the medieval Catholic Church. The number of feast days and holy days was reduced. The nature (and number) of the sacraments was questioned, as well as the appropriateness of the use of images in worship. The Puritans went further than other Reformation groups, however, in their condemnation of images, elimination of *all* feast days, and their prohibition of play and sport even on Sundays. As we have seen, the Puritan work ethic played a significant role in shaping their attitudes toward play. The Puritans regarded play with suspicion and even associated it with sin, primarily because it led the believer away from his or her work. The subsequent American tendency to view work as related to ultimate values has led to the marginalization of play in the culture. As one nineteenth-century visitor from England said, the national motto seemed to be "All work and no play." This heritage still influences us today. Indeed, the play element is in danger of disappearing from sport itself, and even from youth sport in our own context.

The Catholic Church was changing in significant ways as we entered the modern world. Already in the late sixteenth century, there was a new concern on the part of clerical elites with rooting out all "pagan" elements from festival life, and with purity in one's moral life, especially in the area of sexuality. Theologians were preoccupied with the challenges that had been posed by the Reformation, the development of the sciences, and the Enlightenment and spent most of their time developing systematic answers to such challenges.

The elite reform movements in Protestant and Catholic contexts and the dualism of body and soul of the modern world are associated with excarnation—a process wherein the spiritual life is steadily disembodied and comes to be understood as taking place primarily "in the head." This development influenced Catholic theologians and church leaders in the modern world. The earlier insistence on the person as unity of soul and body was in danger of giving way in this context to a hierarchical formulation that associated the mind and the soul with the church and material things and the body with the world. In a more general sense, the reactionary approach of the Catholic Church to so many of the developments of the modern world meant that theologians were not in the habit of respectful dialogue and engagement with various aspects of culture, including games and sport. This lack of engagement is very evident in the U.S. context.

## CHAPTER TWO

# "THE EARTH IS SHAKING WITH FLYING FEET"

As noted in the previous chapter, Christians in the medieval period participated in games and sports as a matter of course on the feast days and holy days of the church year and on Sundays. Humanists and early Jesuits included games and sport as part of the activities of the students in their schools. This could have happened only with the emergence of a particular kind of religious culture. In fact, it was the *way* of being religious—including attitudes about the material world and the body, and the relationship between faith and culture—that led to games and sports being incorporated into the religious calendar of feast days and holy days. These things are discussed more extensively in the next two chapters. For now, let us consider the games and sports of the medieval period and of the humanists and early Jesuits themselves.

## MEDIEVAL PRACTICES

The extent to which games and sports were an integral part of life in medieval and early modern Catholic societies can be glimpsed in two sources that depict life in London from the twelfth to the sixteenth centuries. The first source is subdeacon William Fitzstephen's twelfth-century "Description of London," which includes a section on the sports of the people of London.[1]

John Stow, writing in *A Survey of London* (1598), confirms that most of the games and sports that Fitzstephen discussed had been practiced for four long centuries and had continued up until his own time.[2]

For Fitzstephen, faithful Christian observance and engagement in pastimes and sports naturally go together. In fact, his discussion of the play and games of Londoners is found at the beginning of a book written for religious edification: a biography of Thomas Becket, the recently murdered archbishop of Canterbury. Fitzstephen begins by telling the reader, among other things, that London is a city "happy in its observance of Christian practice" and "cheerful in its sports."[3] He spends a fair amount of time emphasizing the devout character of London's citizens, pointing out that in the city itself, and its suburbs, are thirteen greater, conventual churches and 126 lesser parish churches. He comments, "I do not think there is a city with a better record for church-going, keeping feast-days, giving alms and hospitality to strangers" and other such religious activities. The only problems known in London, according to Fitzstephen, are the immoderate drinking of some people and the frequency of fires. In his view, the sports of the city are for enjoyment, "for it is not fitting that a city should be merely useful and serious-minded, unless it be also pleasant and cheerful."[4]

After Fitzstephen tells the reader that "London provides plays of a more sacred character" in which the miracles of saints or sufferings of the martyrs are presented, he writes in a matter-of-fact manner about the playing of different games and sports on the feast days and holy days of the church year. He describes the games and sports that take place, for example, "on feast days throughout the summer...," "in winter on almost every feast-day before dinner...," "every Sunday in Lent after dinner...," and "at the Easter festival...."[5]

He tells the reader that "every year on the day called

Carnival," the school boys bring fighting cocks to their teachers and spend the whole morning watching the cocks engage in battle. After dinner on Carnival, all the young men go out into the fields to play a ball game. This game must have been very common, because Fitzstephen points out that "the scholars of the various schools have their own ball, and almost all the followers of each occupation have theirs also." The elderly citizens and fathers of the young men, as well as the wealthy magnates of the city, came out on horseback to watch the game "and in their turn to recover their lost youth: the motions of their natural heat seem to be stirred in them at the mere sight of such strenuous activity and by their participation in the joys of unbridled youth."[6]

Figure 1. Fourteenth-Century Stained-Glass Image of a "Golfer." Gloucester Cathedral, England.

"At the Easter festival," Fitzstephen tells the reader, "they play at a kind of naval warfare." As with young people today, this kind of playing at war games was common during the medieval period. While such games provided benefits to a society in need of defense, they were also, judging from Fitzstephen's descriptions, a good deal of fun. In one game, "tilting at the quintain," the goal of a young man riding in the boat was to strike a shield, called the *quintain*, with his lance and break the lance so that he could remain standing in the boat. If the lance did not break, the pressure would thrust him off the back of the boat and into the water. Two other boats carried others ready to rescue him if he was tossed overboard. "On the bridge and the terraces fronting the river stand the spectators," Fitzstephen writes, "ready to laugh their fill."[7]

Some of the activities that Fitzstephen describes we might refer to simply as "play" because they are engaged in for the sheer fun of it but are not contests of a physical nature. When the great marsh to the north of the city freezes over in the winter time, for example, Fitzstephen writes:

> swarms of young men issue forth to play games on the ice. Some, gaining speed in their run, with feet well set apart, slide sideways over a vast expanse of ice. Others make seats out of a large lump of ice, and whilst one sits thereon, others with linked hands run before and drag him along behind them. So swift is their sliding motion that sometimes their feet slip, and they all fall on their faces. Others, more skilled at winter sports, put on their feet the shin-bones of animals, binding them firmly around their ankles, and, holding poles shod with iron in their hands, which they strike from time to time against the ice, they are propelled swift as a bird in flight or a bolt shot from an engine of war.

This play on the ice soon turns into a contest, however, when "by mutual consent, two of them run against each other in this way from a great distance, and, lifting their poles, each tilts against the other."[8]

"On feast-days throughout the summer," Fitzstephen writes that the young men indulged in the sports of archery, running, jumping, wrestling, slinging the stone, hurling the javelin beyond a mark, and fighting with sword and buckler. On these same days, the young women participated in dances led by Cytherea (another name for the Greek goddess Aphrodite), "and until the moon rises, the earth is shaking with flying feet."[9]

John Stow, writing in the late sixteenth century, reports that "these or the like exercises" had continued until his time. He mentions that the stage plays continued without interruption. These sometimes lasted several days and were attended by "most part of the nobility and gentry of England." The cockfights continued and had since become popular occasions for the wagering of money. Ball games were played by people of lower classes in open fields and on the streets and by the nobility on tennis courts. "On the holy days in summer, the youths of this city have in the field exercised themselves in leaping, dancing, shooting, wrestling, casting of the stone or ball, &c."[10]

Figure 2. Fourteenth-Century Misericord with
Two Ball Players. Gloucester Cathedral, England.

Tilting at the quintain now took place on land, and it had changed considerably. The shield itself would now move when the person struck it, and a bag of sand was attached opposite the shield. If the tilter missed the shield, he had failed. But if he struck it, the bag of sand would swing around and hit him from behind, unless he was able to run or ride off (if playing on

31

horseback) fast enough to avoid the blow. This new wrinkle tested the person's agility and speed and also seems to have made tilting more interesting and fun to watch for spectators.

> This exercise of running at the quintain was practiced by the youthful citizens, as well in summer as in winter, namely, in the feast of Christmas, I have seen a quintain set upon Cornhill, by the Leadenhall, where the attendants on the lords of merry disports have run, and made great pastime; for he that hit not the broad end of the quintain was of all men laughed to scorn, and he that hit it full, if he rid not the faster, had a sound blowe in his neck, with a bag full of sand hung on the other end.[11]

According to Stow, with the emergence of the nobility as a separate class, the people of London continued with their sport and recreation and even created new customs. With regard to "sports and pastimes yearly used" for the celebration of Christmas, every noble household, "whether spiritual or temporal"—including that of the king—had "a lord of misrule, or master of merry disports who made the rarest pastimes to delight the Beholders."[12]

> These lords beginning their rule on Alhollon eve, continued the same till the morrow after the Feast of Purification, commonly called Candlemas day. In all which space there were fine and subtle disguisings, masks and mummeries, with playing at cards for counters, nails, and points, in every house, more for pastimes than for gaine.[13]

According to Stow's description of May games, "every parish" was deeply involved in the pastimes and recreation:

> I find also, that in the month of May, the citizens of London of all estates, lightly in every parish, or some-

times two or three parishes joining together, had their several mayings, and did fetch in maypoles, with diverse warlike shows, with good archers, moriss dancers, and other devices, for pastime all the day long, and toward the evening they had stage plays, and bonfires in the streets....[14]

Figure 3. Fourteenth-Century Misericord with Equestrian Falconer. Gloucester Cathedral, England.

Stow tells the reader that he has witnessed a significant change happen in his own lifetime in the sixteenth century in that these pastimes and sports that were common in his youth were now beginning to be suppressed. The "great mayings and May-games," for example, "have not been so freely used as before."[15] In his view, such a development would only lead to greater social problems, because "worse practices within doors are to be feared."[16]

As the feast days and holy days of the medieval period were being left behind in favor of a six-day workweek, some people attempted to continue their pastimes and sports on Sunday, much to the dismay of the Puritans. Philip Stubbes, for example, expressed concern in 1583 about how some people spend the Sabbath:

In maintaining lords of misrule (for so they call a certain kind of play which they use) May games, church ales, feasts and wakes: in bear-baiting, cock fighting, hawking, hunting, and such like. In keeping of fairs and markets on the Sabbath…in football-playing, and such other devilish pastimes…[17]

Such attitudes began to influence how some Christians in England thought about games and sport and would later become commonplace among the Puritans in the early colonies of North America.

While there were regional differences throughout Europe in the medieval period, people in all parts of Europe participated in games and sports on feast days and Sundays. Natalie Zemon Davis lists some of the activities found "in all the cities of France, and indeed of Europe" in the later Middle Ages and the sixteenth century:

> Dancing, music-making, the lighting of fires; reciting of poetry, gaming and athletic contests—the list in all its forms and variations would be longer than the 81 games in Bruegel's famous painting or the 217 games that Rabelais gave to Gargantua. They took place at regular intervals, and whenever the occasion warranted it; they were timed to the calendar of religion and season (the twelve days of Christmas, the days before Lent, early May, Pentecost, the feast of Saint Jean Baptiste in June, the Feast of the Assumption in mid-August, and All Saints) and timed also to domestic events, marriages, and other family affairs.[18]

Davis points out that, aside from the feast of fools, which was sponsored by clerics, "virtually all of the popular recreations were initiated by laymen." These recreations were not official events of the city as were the great Entry parades (parades that were held when a ruler or his representative entered a city). Rather, they were put on by informal circles of family and friends or by crafts of professional guilds and organizations that literary historians have called "societes joyeuses," "fool societies," or "play-acting societies." They called themselves Abbeys of Misrule.[19]

Figure 4. Book of Hours with Ball Players, circa 1300, Franco-Flemish.

Historians of sport have only recently begun to explore the medieval period in any depth, and it is even more recently that they have begun to study women's sports in this period. In the process, enough evidence is appearing, according to Allen Guttmann, "to disprove the dismal null hypothesis about play's total absence from the lives of medieval women." Medieval peasant women's place was not yet exactly in the home, since they participated in the labor of the agrarian economy which, according to Guttmann, "made them a hardy lot."[20] They played football on Shrove Tuesday, as in England, where the married women played the maidens and spinsters. Milkmaids and other girls also played Shrovetide stool-ball, a game where the ball is thrown by one player and hit by another with a bat, prefiguring our modern cricket and baseball. As William Baker writes, "Although modern baseball is primarily American, urban, and male, its roots are medieval, English, rural and female."[21] Cheered on by their families, they participated in foot races on other feast days for prizes such as a smock or piece of cloth. Aristocratic women hunted. In fact, from 1390 to 1830 field sports in England were reserved, by game laws, to "Lords and Ladies." In the later medieval period, the game of court or royal tennis came into favor. The game was probably played predominantly by men, but there is some evidence that women also played, and that they sometimes beat the men. In the *Journal d'un Bourgeois de Paris* of 1427, a Parisian burgher wrote about one Margot of Hainault, who had come to town and bested the men at their favorite pastime.[22]

Figure 5. Blind Man's Bluff in a Medieval Garden.

As one can see, the games and sports of both men and women took place on Sundays and on the feast days and holy days of the church year during the medieval period. They were also depicted in religious art that was used for prayer and worship. As Allen Guttmann says, "The visual record—illuminated manuscripts, stained-glass windows, the carved figures that adorned the great Gothic cathedrals—has proven to be especially important for the glimpses it provides into medieval women's sports."[23] This fact suggests that, for the artists and sculptors of this period and the ordinary churchgoers, games and sports—of both men and women—were not viewed as problematic from a religious point of view. On the contrary, people seemed to understand activities of daily life of this kind to be worthy of a place in the prayer and worship of the community.

## HUMANIST AND EARLY JESUIT PRACTICES

In this section the humanists of Italy and France and the early Jesuits are discussed. The term *humanism* refers to an educational and cultural movement in western Europe in the fourteenth to sixteenth centuries that emphasized the reading of the literary works of antiquity. A *humanist* was an aficionado and teacher of these literary works.[24] The Jesuits (also known as the Society of Jesus) are a religious order of priests and brothers, founded in 1540 by Ignatius of Loyola. They are well known for their work in education and the missions. The humanists and early Jesuits were the first groups in Western Christianity to run schools that were primarily for the education of lay people rather than clerics.

Choosing these two groups makes sense, first of all, because they were Catholic.[25] Ever since Jacob Burckhardt published *The Civilization of the Renaissance in Italy*, there has been a tendency to downplay the religious faith of the humanists and to focus primarily on their role as forerunners of the modern secular world. But to overlook their religious faith is to misunderstand them; most were devout Christians.[26] The Jesuits are a more obvious choice in this regard, as they are recognized perhaps more than any other group as representatives of the Catholic Church in the early modern period. They would have as much influence on Catholicism in the United States as any other group that could have been chosen. It makes sense to treat these two groups together, because of the influence the humanists had on the Jesuit approach to education.

Choosing the humanists and early Jesuits also makes sense because their insistence that games, physical education, and sport be a part of the school day has had such a significant impact on education. The Jesuits, in particular, brought these educational traditions to the United States and would have a significant influence on Catholic schools in this context that has lasted until the present day.

Focusing on the humanists and early Jesuits means that women's experiences will be slighted because they were marginal to the humanist educational enterprise, and they did not attend the early Jesuit schools. This should not be taken to mean that women were not active in games and sports during the early modern period. In fact, according to Allen Guttmann, we know that women continued to play games and sports, as they had during the medieval period. From the fourteenth to the sixteenth centuries, women played football and stool-ball and routinely participated in foot races in many parts of Europe. In Italy, where humanist education began, we know there were running competitions for women during this period in Florence, Brescia, Rome, and Verona. In Venice, where nautical sports had a place of special importance, the women officially started participating in the regatta in 1493.[27]

Very little research has been done on women's sports in continental Europe during the early modern period, however. Because England is widely regarded as the birthplace of modern sports, historians of sport have focused on England during this time period, attempting to understand the transition from traditional to modern forms of sport. For the European continent, however the "documentation is poor for men's sports and worse for women's."[28]

> Almost no one has investigated the archival and published materials in order to discover what early modern upper-class and middle-class girls and women actually did under the rubric of physical education, and even fewer historians have troubled themselves about girls' and women's sports (as opposed to calisthenics). Once we leave England and cross the Channel, sports historians are confronted with another example of women's oft-lamented "invisibility." We know more about the sports of Roman women in the first century A.D. than in the seventeenth and eighteenth centuries.[29]

But it must be acknowledged that, given the focus on England and North America, the men in continental Europe during the seventeenth and eighteenth centuries are somewhat invisible as well. Thus, considering the humanists and early Jesuits can add something important to our knowledge of the history of sport and, in particular, of Catholic attitudes and practices in relation to this aspect of culture. Future research on girls' schools run by the Ursuline sisters in France, and subsequently in America, will help scholars address the "invisibility" of girls and women during this period. As John O'Malley points out, the Ursulines were running more schools for girls in France by the end of the seventeenth century than the Jesuits were for boys.[30]

## THE HUMANIST SCHOOLS

The humanist schools, which had their origins in late fourteenth-century Italy, differed from medieval schools in the extent to which they emphasized the reading of the classic literature of Greek and Roman antiquity. Something that is commonly overlooked in the history of ideas is just how much attention the Greek and Latin authors give to the body, and games and sports, in their writings about education. In the fourth century BCE, Isocrates mentions that his Greek ancestors had invented two disciplines and handed them down to his generation: physical training for the body, of which gymnastics is a part, and philosophy for the soul.

> These two disciplines are complementary, interconnected, and consistent with each other, and through them those who have mastered them make the soul more intelligent and the body more useful. They do not separate these two kinds of education but use similar methods of instruction, exercise, and other kinds of practice.[31]

This approach to education, in which physical and intellectual instruction and exercise went hand in hand, is evident in the schools run by Plato and Aristotle and their successors, in which physical education, athletic contests, and philosophy lessons took place in one *gymnasion-palaistra* complex.[32]

Indeed, the classical authors of Greece and Rome tended to view games and sport simply as a part of life and took for granted that they would be a part of the educational enterprise. Some took things even further, however. Plato, for example, thought play was associated with the sacred. It was important, from his point of view, to be serious with what is truly serious. And for him, "God alone is worthy of supreme seriousness."

> But man is God's plaything, and that is the best part of him. Therefore every man and woman should live life accordingly, and play the noblest games and be of another mind from what they are at present....For they

deem war a serious thing, though in war there is neither play nor culture worthy the name, which are the things *we* deem most serious. Hence all must live in peace as well as they possibly can. What, then, is the right way of living? Life must be lived as play, playing certain games, making sacrifices, singing and dancing, and then a man will be able to propitiate the gods, and defend himself against his enemies and win in the contest.[33]

These emphases of classical authors were not lost on the humanists, who made a vocation of poring over the ancient texts and considering their relevance for the educational programs they were initiating. Nor were they lost on the humanists' students.

The school established in 1423 at the Court of Mantua by Vittorino da Feltre at the request of the Marquis of Mantua was one of the most influential of the early humanist schools. Vittorino named the school building, an old stately villa house donated by the Marquis, "La casa Giocosa," or the Joyful House. He ordered that paintings of children at play be hung throughout the house and also incorporated games and sports into each day's activities. The house was surrounded with extensive grassy fields, "highly prized by Vittorino, who made much use of [them] as playing fields."[34] In the summer, because of the heat, there were trips to villas owned by the Marquis at Goito, or at Borgoforte, or to the Lake of Garda, or the lower Alps of the Veronese. "He always paid serious attention to the health of the scholars," William Harrison Woodward writes of Vittorino. "There was ample space for games, riding, running, and all the athletic exercises then popular. We hear that he specially encouraged certain games at ball, leaping and fencing."[35]

Life at court in late medieval Europe had already included components of physical training, and so the court atmosphere itself of Vittorino's school supported the inclusion of games and sports in the students' school day. Not all the students at Vittorino's school or the later humanist schools, however, were preparing for careers at court. Some were town dwellers or youth of private station and others were poor youth admitted without charge. Vittorino played an important role in the history of education by making the games and physical exercises a part of the school day for all students. As Burkhardt puts it, "Gymnastics as an art, apart both from military training and from mere amusement, was probably first taught by Vittorino da Feltre and after his time became essential to a complete education."[36]

The humanists' approach to education was influenced by the ancient notion that moderation was central to a life of virtue. For Aristotle, virtue lay in the middle—in what he called the "mean"—between the extremes of excess and deficiency. But for him there was a mean with respect to the object and one with respect to the person. He gives the example of ten being too many and two being too few of some object. In this case, six is the mean with respect to the object itself, arrived at by arithmetical reasoning. But there is also a mean in relation to the person, which might very well be different. This mean is decided upon by taking into consideration the person in question and the details of his or her situation in life. "In this way, then, every knowledgeable person avoids excess and deficiency, but looks for the mean and chooses it—not the mean of the thing, but the mean relative to us."[37]

This kind of reasoning was applied by the humanists to their deliberations about the amount of time their young students should devote to their academic pursuits. They often expressed the view that their students should not be spending so much time on their studies that they become exhausted or worn down, which would lead them to regard school as a burden. Rather, they should take a break from their studies from time to time and engage in relaxing activities that would rejuvenate them. Ball games and other sports were understood to be activities of this kind. Aeneas Sylvius Piccolomini, the future Pope Pius II, wrote in a treatise about education for the still very young King Ladislaus of Austria, Hungary, and Bohemia, for example:

> I approve of and praise your playing ball with boys your own age....There is the hoop; there are other perfectly respectable boyish games, which your teachers should sometimes allow you for the sake of relaxation and to stimulate a lively disposition. One should not always be intent on schooling and serious affairs, nor should huge tasks be imposed upon boys, for they may be crushed with exhaustion by such labors, and in any case if they feel overcome by irksome burdens they may be less receptive to learning.[38]

The humanist educator Pier Paolo Vergerio was of the same mind as Piccolomini. For Vergerio, the student should not always be engaged in serious schoolwork "but must from time to time indulge in relaxation."[39] He refers to Quintus Mucius Scaevola, a Roman jurist of the first century and later proconsular governor of Asia and pontifex maximus, who used to take a break from the practice of law by playing a ball game.

> He is said to have been an excellent ball player, a recreation he used to take up particularly to restore his powers and strengthen his chest when tired from the law courts and from his labors in interpreting civil law. A devotion to hunting, fowling and fishing also falls into this category; such activities refresh the spirit with great delight and the movement and effort they require strengthen the limbs, "with zeal gently deceiving severe labor," as Horace says.[40]

The students could learn from this example that recreation was important during their school days but they would also be encouraged to regard it as an important part of a life of moderation in their adult lives as well.

The humanists also made use of the doctrine of the mean in relation to the person when making decisions about *the manner and extent to which* their students should participate in games and sports. They emphasized that the games and exercises should be introduced gradually and by degrees so that they corresponded to the natural dispositions and the physical capacities of each student, which would differ at different ages. Pier Paolo Vergerio wrote in his treatise on education, for example:

> Those exercises, then, should be undertaken which preserve good health and render the limbs more robust; here the natural disposition of each student must be kept in mind....Age must be taken into account, so that up until the age of puberty they should be subjected to lighter burdens, lest the sinews be worn down, even at this age, or the growth of the body impeded. But after puberty they should be broken to heavier tasks....[41]

The humanists in Italy led the way in introducing games and sports into the school days of the children and reflecting on their meaning in their writings on education.[42] But other humanists throughout Europe were also influenced by the ancient authors and were eager to follow the lead of their Italian predecessors. The sixteenth-century French philosopher Michel de Montaigne, for example, wrote in an essay on the education of children:

> It is amazing how concerned Plato is in his Laws with the amusements and pastimes of the youths of his City

44

and how he dwells on their races, sports, singing, capering and dancing, the control and patronage of which has been entrusted, he said, in antiquity to the gods, to Apollo, the Muses and Minerva. His care extends to over a hundred precepts for his *gymnasia*, yet he spends little time over booklearning....[43]

Montaigne was influenced in particular by Plato's tendency to emphasize the unity of body and soul in his writings on education. Reflecting on humanist education in his own time, he wrote:

We are not bringing up a soul; we are not bringing up a body: we are bringing up a man. We must not split him into two. We must not bring up one without the other, but as Plato said, lead them abreast like a pair of horses harnessed together to the same shaft. And does not Plato when you listen to him appear to devote more time and care to exercising the body, convinced that the mind may be exercised with the body, but not vice versa?[44]

In Montaigne's vision, the exercise of the body and soul would occur together because the games and sports would be an integral part of the activities the students were engaged in during a typical day.

The games and sports themselves will form a good part of his studies: racing, wrestling, music making, dancing, hunting and the handling of arms and horses. I want his outward graces, his social ease and his physical dexterity to be molded step by step with his soul.[45]

Montaigne's attitude toward games and sport is the same as the attitude he takes toward other aspects of culture, such as the theater. He recalls fondly his own participation in plays as a young actor and points out that in Greece even gentlemen could make acting their profession. He disagreed with those in his own day who condemned the theater. In his view, civic leaders should foster the stage, as well as games and sport, because these activities help to strengthen a sense of community and good will:

> Those who condemn such entertainments I have even accused of a lack of perspicacity; and of injustice, those who deny entry into our goodly towns to worthwhile troops of actors, begrudging the people such public festivities. Good governments take the trouble to bring their citizens together and to assemble them for sports and games just as they do for serious acts of worship: a sense of community and good-will is increased by this.[46]

## EARLY JESUIT SCHOOLS

According to Philippe Aries, the early Jesuits also played an important role in introducing games and sports as a part of the school day in the Western world. He writes in the book *Centuries of Childhood: A Social History of Family Life* that the understanding of the place of games and physical education for children in schools was modified in the course of the seventeenth century "largely owing to the influence of the Jesuits."[47] According to Aries:

> The Fathers realized from the start that it was neither possible nor even desirable to suppress them or to make them dependent on occasional, precarious and shameful permission. They proposed to assimilate them, to introduce them officially into their curricula

46

and regulations, on condition that they chose and controlled them.[48]

Francois de Dainville notes in his book, *L'Education des Jesuites: XVI–XVIII siecles*, that the early Jesuits in France found out soon after opening their schools that requiring the young students to study for too long was not good for the health of the students. Because the long hours in the classroom were unnatural for younger children, the teachers would also become exhausted trying to enforce discipline. Based in part on these experiences, the Jesuits gradually reduced the amount of time students were in classes each day from six and a half to five hours. An hour of recreation was introduced following the noon meal and three-quarters of an hour after other meals. "A little bit of recreation" was introduced between the classes.[49]

Dainville also points out that the early Jesuits adjusted the weekly schedule to allow time for physical recreation and sport. They introduced one free day in the middle of the week, usually on Wednesday or Thursday. On this day, the students would take a walk into the countryside. The whole point of this outing was to give the students a chance to get some physical exercise, which included the playing of games and sports. The young Jesuits in training who taught the students were encouraged to "join the crowd" on these occasions, and it is reported that they "joyfully obliged."[50] These young Jesuits, while participating in the recreational walks, were supposed to make sure that the games didn't become too violent, and were supposed to watch out especially for the youngest students, so that their health was not endangered in any way.

During the summer months, this exercise walk took place between six and nine o'clock in the morning. The rest of the day was spent in the countryside at a villa owned by the Society, playing ball games that were relatively calmer and card games and chess. For the older students, there was a daylong excursion into the countryside twice a year in groups of ten to twelve, either on their own or accompanied by one of the priests. These excursions were eventually scheduled on a monthly basis.[51]

The Jesuits had continued the medieval practice of observing the feast days and the holy days of the church year. In the academic context, the holy day was observed with a vacation day from school. This meant that, occasionally, the students would have two vacation days in the course of a week, the recreation day mentioned earlier and a feast day (depending on when the feast day fell). Such free days were occasions for the students to play various games and sports. The Jesuits also scheduled longer vacations for the students at Christmas, Easter, and in the summer months.

Detailed instructions regarding vacation days and recreation would soon be articulated in the *Ratio Studiorum* of 1599, the formal education program for the Society's schools. "A nice balance should be maintained," the authors of the *Ratio* wrote, "between study time and recreation periods."[52] For this reason, they give much attention to the balance among school days, recreation days, and vacation periods. And their instructions, characteristically, were quite detailed. For instance, they made distinctions between the students on the basis of their age. Generally speaking, vacations and recreation time were longer for older students than for younger students. The older students, it seems, were considered capable of handling more free time, while the younger ones were still thought to benefit from a more structured environment. One reads, for example, that for the Easter break, "in the higher classes there will be vacation from Palm Sunday until Low Sunday [two weeks]; in the lower classes from Wednesday noon on Holy Week till Easter Tuesday [almost one week]."[53]

# "The Earth Is Shaking with Flying Feet"

Dainville points out that the early Jesuits began their schools in France in buildings that were built for other purposes but were not currently being used. These buildings did not have open spaces in which the children could get physical exercise or play sports. The first buildings the Jesuits themselves built in the last third of the sixteenth century, however, were built with spacious courtyards surrounded by classrooms on all sides. The creation of the courtyard in the center of the physical structure of the schools sanctioned and encouraged the playing of active games and sports. The idea initially was that students who lived at the school would use the courtyard in their free time; it became such a popular place, however, that the students who lived at home also used it on a regular basis.[54]

The Jesuits encouraged games that required physical activity and exertion at their schools. This emphasis can be seen in a letter from Francis Borgia, the third superior general of the Jesuits, to the rector at the College d'Aquitaine in 1568. The rector had described to Borgia the situation at the college with respect to games and sports and asked for his counsel. In his response, Borgia wrote that while one ought not forbid board games like chess or checkers, neither was it necessary to encourage them. He thought rather that "the best games are those which entail some physical exercise, such as the game where one launches a ball into an iron ring with a mallet."[55]

Following the example of Borgia, whom Dainville calls "the saint who was the great initiator of recreation in our system of education,"[56] subsequent formal visitors of the Society to the schools regularly encouraged active games. In their ordinances, they emphasized that the hours and days set aside for recreation should not be passed interminably with board games like chess or checkers or become hidden extensions of study—as some students tended to make them. This emphasis

49

on active games and sports, Dainville points out, was in line with the approach of Cardinal Antonanio, who had written:

> The lively and mobile spirit of children demands a lot of movement. This agitation is very helpful for them. It excites and develops natural warmness (inner fire). Their members, exercised by a race, by jumping and by rapid movements become agile, supple and robust. Children and youth shouldn't therefore ordinarily choose tranquil games; they need some vigorous exercise, such as the game of ball, for example, which is strongly praised by physicians.[57]

According to Dainville, the face of recreation changed in important ways in the latter part of the sixteenth century in Jesuit schools and French society more broadly due to these new emphases. Games that required much vigor and intense physical activity became the norm. Ball games like *la choule*, a precursor of soccer, and *la paume*, an early form of tennis, pall mall,[58] and running contests were most common. Dainville points out that one can get a sense of the intensity with which the students would play these games at the Jesuit schools because of the frequency with which the soles of their shoes had to be replaced. Such details are found in the accounting books of the schools.[59]

According to Dainville, the approach to games and physical recreation described above was still operative in the Jesuit schools in France when the Society was suppressed in 1773. Although some say that there was a "softening of body and soul" in French society in the eighteenth century, Dainville reports that there was still much sporting activity in the Jesuit colleges during this period. As a young Jesuit who taught at the College Louis Le Grand in the eighteenth century observed:

If children are in the courtyard they are in "liberty land". They are there on the free days during the entire day, from 9:00 to 6:00, only stopping at meal time. It would be against the good order of the college to get somebody out of this except for health reasons. And free days are countless, coming nearly every Tuesday and Thursday in the year.[60]

The Jesuits not only *allowed* the students to play games in their schools, however. They published Latin treatises giving rules for the recommended games. These treatises had an important influence on later developments in French society. According to Aries, "The doctors of the eighteenth century, taking as their inspiration the old 'exercise games' in the Jesuits' Latin treatises, elaborated a new technique of bodily hygiene: physical culture."[61] Jean Pierre de Crousaz, a professor of philosophy and mathematics at Lausanne, for example, wrote in his *Traite de l'education des enfants* in 1722, "While it is growing, it is essential for the human body to be greatly agitated....I consider games affording exercise to be preferable to all others."[62] Joseph-Clement Tissot's *Gymnastique medicale et chirurgicale* recommends active games as the best form of recreation: "They exercise all the parts of the body at the same time...quite apart from the fact that the action of the lungs is constantly stimulated by the shouts and calls of the players."[63]

This section of the chapter has been informed by the research of Francois de Dainville and has focused primarily on Jesuit schools in France. But a very similar approach was taken with respect to games and sports in most of the nearly eight hundred schools that the Jesuits were operating at the time of their suppression in the late eighteenth century. As one historian put it with respect to the schools run by German Jesuits:

It is a well known fact that in Germany sport in the higher schools, is, or was, until recently, neglected more than is expedient for the general development of the pupils. And yet, wherever German Jesuits opened a college, be it in Freiburg (Switzerland), Feldkirch (Vorarlberg), or Sao Leopoldo (Brazil), everywhere they introduced and encouraged plenty of healthful games, an evident sign that it is the spirit of the Society to give the pupils sufficient recreation.[64]

The similarity in approaches was due in large part to the involvement of the major superiors of the order, including the superior general, in decisions that were being made regarding games and sports in the schools and the publication of the *Ratio Studiorum*, which contained mandates for recreation, vacation days, and so on, for all of the Society's schools.

# INFLUENCES ON THE EARLY JESUITS

The approach of the Jesuits working in the schools was influenced by the sensibilities of Ignatius of Loyola, the founder of the order. Ignatius learned a great deal about the importance of moderation and taking care of the body from his own life experience. When he embarked on a new life path after being injured by a cannonball at Pamplona, he took up excessive fasts and penances, which left him with stomach ailments the rest of his life. This led him to emphasize to other Jesuits the importance of moderation in fasting, and spiritual exercises in general. In a 1548 letter to Francis Borgia, for example, he encourages him to reduce by half the time he alots to prayer and fasting.

In as much as both soul and body are your Creator and Lord's, you must give him a good accounting of the whole and hence not let the bodily nature become weakened; for if it is weak, the inward nature will no longer be able to function properly. Consequently, while I did strongly commend the fasts, rigorous abstinence, and retrenchment from ordinary food, and for a time was quite glad about them, I can no longer do so now that I see that these fasts and abstinences keep the stomach from functioning naturally and from digesting ordinary meats or other foods which supply proper sustenance to the body. Instead, I would seek every possible means to strengthen the body, eating any permissible foods and [doing so] as frequently as you find them beneficial....[65]

It seems that Borgia was slow to learn this lesson. In 1555 Ignatius felt the need to write to him again, indicating that he had learned from other Jesuits that "you do not treat yourself —your body, I mean—with the same charity you show toward others. You eat badly, overwork, and you do not let others assist you."[66] He put Borgia under the direction of another Jesuit with respect to these matters, to ensure his health and strength, which he felt required "better treatment of the body."[67]

One of the places Ignatius learned about moderation as central to a life of virtue was at the University of Paris, where he was a student from around 1528 to 1536. At Paris, Ignatius would have encountered an Aristotelian understanding of the virtues especially through the writings of Thomas Aquinas, who was heavily indebted to Aristotle's *Nicomachean Ethics* for his own account of the moral life. Ignatius held Thomas in very high regard, as is clear from the fact that he is the only theologian mentioned by name in the part of the *Constitutions* concerning the studies of young Jesuits in training. The emphasis on the study of Thomas in the training of Jesuits would ensure that the

Aristotelian emphasis on moderation would be kept alive in the sensibilities of the future members of the Society of Jesus.

These developments had an impact that went beyond mere theorizing. Ignatius emphasized the importance of moderation with respect to the studies and spiritual exercises of the young Jesuits during their training. The third part of the "Rules of the Colleges" that were written for the first colleges where young Jesuits lived and studied is dedicated to "Conserving the Health and Strength of the Body." Here it is written that "it is necessary to moderate the spiritual exercises, such as devotions and studies, not wanting to do too much in the first days, that one would not be able to last in them."[68] Another part of the same document pertains to

> *Some honest bodily recreation.* There will also be some hours for honest bodily recreation, as after lunch or dinner for a while; between the hours of study some relaxation is as useful for the body as for the studies, to which one returns with more of a disposition to make progress, when preceded by some honest bodily exercise.[69]

Such advice about the studies of young Jesuits also appeared in the *Constitutions* of the order, widening its influence. In this document, Ignatius writes, "Special attention should be given to their abstaining from studies at times inopportune for bodily health, to their taking sufficient sleep, and to their observance of moderation in mental labors..." and that "it is not good to continue to work for a long time without some proper relaxation or recreation."[70]

Ignatius had also established an important precedent by purchasing a villa house outside of Rome in the early years of the Society.[71] Some Jesuits living in Rome at the time objected to this purchase because they thought the Society did not have enough money to buy the country estate. They were also concerned about the possibility of dissolute behavior at the villa, which they thought would provide a bad example for future members of the Society. But Ignatius thought that it was necessary to have a place where future Jesuits could go to relieve the stress of work and mental labors by taking some recreation and rest. He also thought that if the rules were clearly stated from the start, problems having to do with dissolute behavior would be less likely. Goncalves da Camara writes in his *Memoriale* that "for this reason he wanted criteria to be laid down now about what should be done in this regard, and that the first should provide a rule and example for those coming after them."[72]

> In order to do this he himself indicated and arranged those games that the brethren might play at the country house, which were only the tablet game and the quoit or target game. The first was in imitation of the College of the Sorbonne, which is the most important in Paris and has the most learned and dedicated members. There the teachers are accustomed to play a game after dinner with the keys of their rooms: whoever gets nearest the edge of the table wins. And instead of the keys, our Father ordered the tablets, which we still use now. For the second game he had some thin iron round disks made, about a palm's width wide, with a large hole in the middle for the fingers to fit in easily. With his own hand he made a model out of red wax of the size he wanted.[73]

The important role that the principle of moderation played in the thinking of Jesuits about games and sport can be seen in the writings of the seventeenth-century Jesuit Francois Pierron. For Pierron, life in civil society would be somber and boring without games and recreation. "Recreations are called such," he wrote in *Le Bon Precepteur*, "because they give new being to spirits which are overwhelmed by too much work."[74] For Pierron, work should not and cannot be continued without ceasing, and if a person works very seriously at their tasks, "it is very reasonable that one would enjoy some rest from time to time, and that one would take some recreation."[75] But all the same, it was important that the games themselves be approached with moderation. "Be on your guard," Pierron wrote. "If you love your life, moderate your desires."[76] After all, as he put it, "the games which are not moderated by discretion are accompanied and followed by many great misfortunes."[77]

# THE JESUIT MISSIONS

The sensibilities concerning games and sports of the Jesuits working in schools were similar to those of the early Jesuit missionaries to the Native peoples of North America. This is not surprising given that the missionaries themselves had attended the Jesuits schools in France described in the previous section; they received a classical education and played active games and sports as a matter of course during their youth. Their training in philosophy and theology in the Society also introduced them to the Aristotelian notion of moderation as central to the life of virtue.

According to the reports of the Jesuit missionaries, the games of the Native Americans were woven into the fabric of their daily lives and simply taken for granted. Father Paul du Ru observes a kind of ball game among the Muskogeans in Mississippi, for example:

> 27 February, 1700: We walked to the village where there were games and a great dance. The men play in pairs; one of them has a ball in his hand and throws it ahead.

Both of them run as fast as they can, throwing a big stick after this ball and, as well as I could make out, the one whose stick is closest to the ball wins the play. Then the one who wins throws the ball the next time. This is a rather strenuous game: nevertheless, it is played by both old and young.[78]

The women also played ball games. Father du Ru comments:

The women have a game also. They separate into two parties between two large posts in the square. Somebody throws a little ball in the center, and the one who seizes it first tries her best to run around the post on her side three times, but she is prevented by the women of the opposite party who seize her if they can. When she can no longer resist them, she throws the ball to her people who make a similar effort to run around their post.... The games are very long and ordinarily when they are over the women plunge into the water to refresh themselves. Sometimes the men play this game also.[79]

Such matter-of-fact descriptions of the games of the Native peoples is common in the correspondence of the early Jesuit missionaries.

In this new context, the games provided the Jesuits with an opportunity to compare the customs of the Native peoples with European customs. In this sense, they were a reminder of our common humanity. Paul Le Jeune writes that there seem to be "certain little games that children find out for themselves without being taught." Hide-and-seek is one example of such a game, he points out. The Natives played a number of other children's games that Le Jeune had noticed in Europe as well. He describes one such game in which the "little Parisians" used to throw a musket ball into the air and catch it with a little bat that was scooped out for this purpose. He comments:

> The little montagnard [mountain] Savages do the same, using a little bunch of Pine sticks, which they receive or throw into the air on the end of a pointed stick. The little Hiroquois have the same pastime, throwing a bone with a hole in it, which they interlace in the air with another little bone. I was told this by a young man of that nation as we were watching the little montagnard children play.[80]

The Jesuits objected to games associated with gambling. They also objected if the games were associated with what they viewed as "superstitious" beliefs. The notion that playing a game had curative powers was a common belief among the Native peoples and was regarded as superstitious and usually condemned by the Jesuits. But not universally so. John de Brebeuf, for example, urges a compassionate attitude toward such practices.

> Circa 1636: Of three kinds of games especially in use among these Peoples, namely, the games of crosse, dish, and straw,—the first two are, they say, most healing. Is this not worthy of compassion? There is a poor sick man, fevered of body and almost dying, and a miserable Sorcerer will order for him, as a cooling remedy, a game of crosse. Or the sick man himself, sometimes, will have dreamed that he must die unless the whole country shall play crosse for his health; and, no matter how little may be his credit, you will see then in a beautiful field, Village contending against Village, as to who will play crosse the better, and betting against one another Beaver robes and Porcelain collars, so as to excite greater interest.

## "The Earth Is Shaking with Flying Feet"

> Sometimes, also, one of these Jugglers will say that
> the whole Country is sick, and he asks a game of crosse
> to heal it; no more needs to be said, it is published
> immediately everywhere....[81]

Even if Brebeuf's view of this cultural and religious practice was not widely shared by other Jesuits, it does illustrate the extent to which some would occasionally go to try to understand and appreciate the Native cultural and spiritual traditions.

Joseph Lafitau wrote at greater length than any of the Jesuits about the games and sports of the Native peoples of North America in his book *Customs of the American Indians Compared with the Customs of Primitive Times*.[82] While Lafitau understood himself primarily as a Jesuit missionary, because of his detailed and careful description of Native American customs and beliefs he is widely regarded as one of the most important figures in the emergence of the academic discipline of anthropology.[83]

For Lafitau, games and sports were worthy of sustained reflection. He writes in the very first lines of the chapter entitled "Games":

> Besides the necessary occupations the Indians have
> others which are either pure diversion, as are their
> games of chance, or diversion mixed with exercise,
> which are in the province of gymnastics, serving to
> exercise and form the body. These games are among
> the first institutions of men, and the first with which
> the ancient authors have acquainted us.[84]

Lafitau points out in the opening sentences of his chapter that the games of the Natives of North America are more ancient than those that Palamedes invented during the siege of

Troy and probably than those invented by the Lydians, who were thought by Europeans—thanks to Herodotus's account in *The Persian Wars*—to be the originators of all sorts of games.[85]

As was mentioned earlier, writing about games and sports was one way that the Jesuits could highlight the common humanity of the Native peoples and the Europeans. Lafitau did just this with respect to games of chance. For Lafitau, it was "one of the greatest pleasures" to watch the Natives play these games because they were so "ardent and animated."

> While one of the players shakes the dish, those who are betting with him cry, all with one voice, repeating incessantly the wish that he makes for the colour and lie of the fruit-stones. All those of the opposite party cry also, on their side demanding the contrary....Both sides...move about so actively that...they are all perspiring as if they had played a hard game of handball or some other vigorous exercise.[86]

He points out the similarities with the ancient Roman games of chance:

> The ancients, when they played their games of chance, moved about as actively as the Indians do today and showed the same vivacity....They demanded in a loud voice the lot which they desired. They shouted and moved about so actively that they poured forth sweat in great drops. A thing which, as Suetonius reports, made Augustus say in writing to Tiberius, "*forum aleatorium calefecimus*" [we heated up the gamesters' forum].[87]

Because Lafitau highlighted the similarities between the experiences of the Native peoples and those described in the classical literature of Western culture, the Native peoples would perhaps not seem quite so distant or exotic to his readers.

## "The Earth Is Shaking with Flying Feet"

After discussing the games of chance, Lafitau discusses ball games, a subject about which he was very knowledgeable.[88] In the context of a discussion of three other kinds of ball games, he discusses the similarities between the Native game of lacrosse and a game played by the ancient Greeks and Romans called *epicyrus* or *harpastum*. The rules of the two games shared many features in common. Readers with even a superficial familiarity with lacrosse will recognize similarities with the rules of epicyrus as described by the ancient writer Pollux, whom Lafitau quotes:

> The players are divided according to their number and distributed into two teams as equal in number as possible. Then a line is drawn in the centre of the field which they call *okuros* on which they put the ball. In the same way, two other lines are drawn, far apart to serve as limits, behind each of these two teams. Those to whom the lot has fallen, first throw the ball towards the opposing side which makes, on its side, every effort to throw it back to where it comes from. The game goes on in this way, until one or the other has driven his adversary to the limit or the line which he is to defend.[89]

Other ancient authors point out that epicyrus or harpastum was played on sand, as was lacrosse. According to Lafitau, this is clear "from the epithet of *poudreux* [dusty] which Martial gives to the *harpastum* every time he speaks of it, as well as that of *aremaria* [sandy] which occurs in St. Isidore of Seville which signifies to us that this ball always rolled in the dust."[90]

Another piece of evidence Lafitau gives that epicyrus or harpastum is the same game as lacrosse is that basically the same game was being played in his own day throughout Europe and in all of the Americas. Since the game as it was currently being played in Europe did not come from the Native people of North America, Lafitau thought that it likely had its origins in epicyrus or harpatus, which was played by Greeks and Romans of the ancient world.

# CONCLUSION

This chapter has shown that games and sports were an important part of Catholic medieval and early modern societies in Europe. People engaged in games and sport on feast days and holy days, and such activities were depicted in prayer books and on stained glass windows and in woodcuts of churches and cathedrals. The humanists and early Jesuits included games and sports as activities for the students in their schools. They were influenced in this regard by the medieval cultural traditions just mentioned and the writings of authors in the classical tradition who emphasized the importance of educating the body and of games and sports in schools. The classical notion that moderation was central to a life of virtue influenced the humanists and the early Jesuits. In this case, moderation meant that the students should not be excessive in the pursuit of their studies or spiritual exercises, but should also take time for relaxation and to be rejuvenated. The games and sports were activities that provided for such relaxation. The Jesuit missionaries also had an accepting attitude toward the games and sports of the Native peoples they were encountering in North America. And the games provided the missionaries with an opportunity to emphasize the common humanity that Native peoples shared with Europeans. If it is true that games and sports had a place of such importance in Catholic medieval and early modern societies, what were the theological and spiritual influences that could have led to the emergence of such societies? The next two chapters consider these questions.

# CHAPTER THREE

# "THE SPIRIT IS BOUND WITH THE FLESH"

## THE BODY IN SPORT:
## A CONTESTED HISTORY

As was noted in chapter 1, a recurring narrative in scholarship on the history of sport tells the story of how Christians up until the time of the Reformation emphasized the importance of the soul and the spiritual realm and regarded the body as unimportant or even as an obstacle in the spiritual life. For some scholars, this was the reason that little importance was given to games and sport during the medieval and early modern periods. According to these accounts, it was only after the repressive regime of the Puritans in England and America that more enlightened views about the body began to take hold. In the nineteenth century, games and sports began to be accepted by reasonable people and to have a more prominent place in society. The suggestion is that Christians and theologians have only recently, and reluctantly, embraced sports.

This narrative, for example, appears in a 1993 essay by D. Stanley Eitzen and George H. Sage about the relationship between sport and religion. These authors write, "Early Christianity gradually built a foundation based on asceticism, which is a belief that evil exists in the body, and therefore, the body should be subordinate to the pure spirit....Nothing could have been more damning for the promotion of active recreation and sport." Until the Reformation, the authors of the essay tell us, "spiritual salvation" was the dominant feature of the Christian faith, which meant that cultivation of the body needed to be subordinated to salvation of the spirit, "especially since the body can obstruct the realization of this aim." The Reformation brought to an end the "vicelike grip that Roman Catholicism had on the minds and habits of the people of Europe and England." The Reformation didn't end the suspicion of sport, however, because the Puritans were "a greater enemy to sport than Roman Catholicism had been." It wasn't until later, in the nineteenth and twentieth centuries, that Protestants in England and North America came to view sport in positive terms and as an instrument to promote the work of the Lord. The attitude of Christians in this more recent period can best be described, these authors say, as "If you can't lick 'em, join 'em!"[1]

For Clifford Putney, Christianity's "traditional mistrust of purely physical enjoyments, and perforce of physical recreation" dates to its inception. The apostle Paul expressed the view in his letter to Timothy that bodily exercise profits little in comparison with godliness, for example. For Putney, Paul viewed corporeal improvements as irrelevant because he thought the second coming was imminent. The postponement of the Parousia, however, did not "sway the Church greatly with regard to the body."

> Indeed, the Church Fathers' discovery of Plato early in the Middle Ages actually intensified their aversion to carnal amusements. Plato...believed this world to be but an imperfect copy of the next. Accordingly, the medieval Church, which incorporated Platonism into its colleges and universities, supported a curriculum wherein physical education mattered little and academic reflection much. Not content with this, the Church also "persistently suppressed many sports and games."[2]

## "The Spirit Is Bound with the Flesh"

Putney argues that Catholic teachings such as these regarding the body and sports reigned supreme until the Reformation. Martin Luther was representative of the more tolerant side of Protestantism, and John Calvin, "who even more passionately than the Catholics felt the flesh to be vile," of the more severe view.[3] According to Putney, it would only be in the late nineteenth and early twentieth centuries that Protestant "muscular Christians" in England and North America would finally embrace sport.

Even Allen Guttmann, who has written extensively about the place of games and sports in the medieval and early modern periods in Europe, tends to characterize the influence of Christianity as a thoroughly negative one. According to him, patristic Christianity was "extremely hostile to sports" partly because it was associated with pagan cult and partly because of "Christianity's dualistic ontology which split the self into mortal body and immortal soul."[4] With regard to the Christians who had been martyred in the Roman arenas, he writes:

> The mortal bodies mangled in the arena were, of course, less prized by the faithful than were the immortal souls they housed. In fact, "house" is too weak a metaphor to express the asceticism that was unquestionably a part of Christian piety. References to the human body as a prison, a charnel house, a grave, or a sink of corruption were ubiquitous in the religious literature of late antiquity and the Middle Ages as ascetic men and women were inspired to join the ranks of "those who made themselves eunuchs for the kingdom of Heaven" (Matt 19:2).[5]

In Guttmann's view, because of their bias against the body, Christians have only lately come around to approving of sport. As he puts it:

After long and stubborn opposition to the allegedly misplaced emphasis on the body symbolized in Greek athletics, both Catholicism and Protestantism have worked out a *modus vivendi*, a kind of concordat, with modern sports. Theologians now repudiate the harsh condemnations of earlier generations and blame Platonism and Neo-Platonism for the ascetic strain in traditional Christianity. Churchmen now seek eagerly to establish the harmony of modern sports and Christian doctrine.[6]

The authors cited tend to seize on some of the more rigorous statements of early Christians regarding the body and sexuality and to present them as representative of the whole of Christianity during that period. Then they assume that these views were the primary influence shaping the sensibilities of Christians in later periods. But this is something that needs to be demonstrated rather than assumed. While it is possible to find examples of early Christians who held severe views regarding the human body and sexuality, it is another matter to determine the kind of influence these views had on Christian sensibilities and religious practices (especially those of lay people) in later periods. Indeed, it is a complicated matter to assess the influences on a religious tradition that spans many centuries and diverse cultures. And such a task requires making use of evidence in a careful and thoughtful way to establish the relationship between historical sources and religious sensibility and practices in different periods.[7]

If one starts with *what people were doing* in the medieval and early modern periods, a different picture emerges from the one described by the authors cited. As mentioned in chapter 1, in the medieval period people went on pilgrimages to sites with the relics of saints, participated in processions, put on mystery and morality plays, crawled to the cross, put ashes on their foreheads, said their rosaries, painted and sculpted scenes from the Bible, read illuminated prayer books, engaged in corporal works of mercy, and participated in the sacraments that made use of bread, wine, oil, fire, and water. As we saw in the chapter 2, people played games and sports as a matter of course and most often in connection with the most important religious celebrations. These games and sport were depicted in prayer books and on stained glass windows and in woodcuts in churches and were later incorporated into the schools of the humanists and early Jesuits. The early Jesuits also made genuine attempts to understand the games and sports of the various cultures they were encountering in their missionary work.

To understand how a religious culture such as *this* emerged in the medieval and early modern periods, the writings of theologians such as Irenaeus, Augustine, Pseudo-Dionysus, John of Damascus, and Thomas Aquinas are most important. These were the most influential theologians during these periods, and each of them held that the material world was good and the human body was constitutive of human identity. It was precisely these convictions that shaped how they wrote about topics such as the sacraments and the use of images in Christian worship and that can help us to understand why the body was so integrally involved in religious practices during these periods.[8] Significantly, these views were endorsed by the formal teaching of the church. One of the things such formal, public declarations do is to set boundaries, in a sense, outside of which one's views were no longer recognizably Christian. This is important because it meant that the "rules" were set in a sense for theologians and priests, and in this case, one of the rules was, "You can't denigrate the human body per se."

The way Sage and Eitzen, Putney, and Guttmann interpret the Christian scriptures and the meaning of the body in the Christian life has been pervasive in the literature on the history of sport. But theirs is not an entirely new interpretation. Groups like the Gnostics, Manicheans, and Cathars and Waldensians all had similar interpretations, each of them teaching that the material world and the human body were associated with evil and were not capable of participating in the life of the Spirit. All of these groups were declared heretical by Christian theologians and the formal teaching of the church for precisely these views.[9]

# THE GNOSTIC CONTROVERSY

One of the central difficulties that early Christians had with the Gnostics was that they did not accept the Hebrew scriptures, or Old Testament, as part of the Christian scriptures. This meant that they did not accept the account of God's creation of the world described in the first chapter of Genesis and the insistence there that the material world is good, indeed "very good." Rather, it was characteristic of Gnostic teaching to distinguish between a remote and unknowable Supreme Being, whom they worshiped, and the "creator god." From the Supreme Being the "creator god" was derived by a series of emanations or aeons. Through "some mischance or fall among the higher aeons,"[10] this creator god was regarded as the immediate source of the material world and governed this world. Because the material world was understood to be the result of an accident or fall, it was viewed as imperfect and "antagonistic to what was truly spiritual."[11] This led the Gnostics to the view, as Irenaeus complains, that "what is material cannot share in salvation, for it is not receptive of it, they say...."[12]

Another common feature of Gnostic teaching was that it removed Jesus Christ from association with the material world. According to this point of view, Jesus did not have a real body, suffer death on a cross, or rise bodily from the dead. "Christ received nothing material," Irenaeus writes, "for the material is not capable of being saved."[13] As Justin Martyr wrote, "And there are some who maintain that even Jesus Himself appeared only as spiritual, and not in the flesh, but presented merely the appearance of flesh: these persons seek to rob the flesh of the promise."[14]

According to the Gnostic view, the Father to whom Jesus referred in his preaching and teaching was the Supreme God above the creator god. Jesus was sent by this Supreme God to bring *gnosis* or awakening to human beings. A few elite people received a divine spark and through gnosis, and the rites associated with it, were rescued from the "evil material environment" and returned to their home in the Divine Being.[15] These people were designated *spiritual*, while others were merely *fleshly* or *material*. Some of the groups added a third category in between these two, the *psychic*, which referred to ordinary churchgoers. The rites that the *spiritual* participated in were not connected to the material things of this world or the human body. Irenaeus writes about Gnostic thinkers who

> say that the mystery of the ineffable and invisible Power should not be performed through created things, visible and perishable, nor that of unthinkable and bodiless realities through sensible and corporeal things....This redemption is neither corporeal, since the body is perishable, nor psychic, since the soul too comes from the deficiency and is like a dwelling for the spirit. Redemption must therefore be spiritual.[16]

Since redemption was *spiritual* for the Gnostics (understood in contrast to the material and the bodily), it should not be surprising to learn that they understood both marriage and procreation to be associated with impurity and evil and regarded them with grave suspicion.

In contrast to these views, Irenaeus, along with other early Christian theologians in the second century, emphasized that God created all things on earth and in heaven, visible and invisible, corporeal and spiritual—and pronounced all things good. He writes in "Against Heresies":

> We hold fast the rule of truth, that there is one almighty God who founded everything through his Word and arranged it and made everything out of the non-existent, as scripture says: "By the Word of the Lord the heavens were made firm and by the Spirit of his mouth all their power," and further, "All things were made through him and without him nothing was made." (Jn 1:3) Nothing is excepted from this "all things." Through him the Father made everything, visible and invisible, sense-perceptible and intelligible, temporal for God's plan or eternal.[17]

The human body, obviously, was included in "all things." As was mentioned earlier, this is why Christians, as Irenaeus put it, "hope for the...salvation of the whole man, that is, of soul and body."[18]

In his writings against the Gnostics, Irenaeus also repeatedly referred to the scriptural accounts about the Word becoming flesh. His theory of recapitulation required that Jesus pass through all of the stages of human life from birth through maturity, undoing the evil at each stage along the way. He writes that Jesus was born of Mary—and received flesh from her:

> And if he had received nothing from Mary he would never have taken foods derived from the earth; after fasting forty days....he would not have felt hunger because his body needed food; John his disciple would

not have written of him: "Jesus sat, wearied from the journey" (Jn 4:6); nor would David have proclaimed, "They have added to the pain of my wounds" (Ps 69:26); he would not have wept over Lazarus (Jn 11:35); he would not have sweated drops of blood (Lk 22:44); he would not have said, "My soul grieves" (Matt 26:38), nor would blood and water have come forth from his pierced side (Jn 19:34). All these are signs of the flesh taken from the earth, which he recapitulated in himself, saving what he had formed.[19]

According to Irenaeus, since human beings, who were lost, were made of flesh and blood, the Word too was made of flesh and blood, recapitulating in himself the original work of creation, "not something different, and seeking what was lost."[20]

Irenaeus's disagreements with the Gnostics about the meaning of the material world and the human body in the Christian life were also rooted in differing interpretations of the writings of the apostle Paul. According to Irenaeus, one of the things the Gnostic writers overlook is that Paul uses the term *flesh* to mean different things at different times. They tended to seize on passages such as "Flesh and blood cannot inherit the kingdom of God" (1 Cor 15:50) and to conclude that Paul regarded the body only in negative terms, as an obstacle in the Christian life. Irenaeus compared them to novice wrestlers who get overly excited about their first move and put everything they have into their opening thrust, thinking it will bring them victory.

It happens that novice wrestlers, struggling with others, forcibly grab a part of their adversary's body and are thrown to the ground by the part they hold; as they fall they suppose they are winning because they vigorously hold that member they first seized, but in fact they are held in derision because they have fallen. Thus, when the heretics take two expressions from Paul, "Flesh and blood cannot inherit the kingdom of God" (1 Cor 15:50), they have not understood the mind of the Apostle or studied the meaning of his expressions. Simply holding to the mere words, they die in relation to them, overturning the whole "economy" of God as far as they can.[21]

According to Irenaeus, Paul is using the phrase "flesh and blood" in the passage from Corinthians to refer to those carnal actions that turn a person toward sin and deprive him of life. He is not saying that the bodily life of human beings per se is at odds with life in the Spirit.

Irenaeus reminds his adversaries that the apostle Paul writes about God setting him apart from his mother's womb (that is, "the ancient substance of the flesh") and calling him through his grace to preach the gospel to the Gentiles. That is, Paul didn't cease being a flesh and blood human being when he became a Christian and a minister of the gospel. "For there was not one born from the womb and another who proclaimed the Son of God," Irenaeus writes, "but the same one formerly ignorant who persecuted the church (Gal 1:13)...when revelation was made to him...preached the Gospel of the Son of God Christ Jesus...."

He also points out that Paul repeatedly uses the word *flesh* to refer to this very Son of God, Christ Jesus.

What proves that it is not the substance of flesh and blood that the Apostle attacks when he says it does not possess the kingdom of God (1Cor 15:50) is the fact that he constantly uses the terms flesh and blood of Our Lord Jesus Christ, sometimes to show that he was

72

a man (for the Lord himself called himself Son of man) and sometimes to confirm the salvation of our flesh.[22]

Irenaeus writes that this same apostle who was born from the womb writes in his letter to the Ephesians that "life in the flesh is a fruitful labor" (Phil 1:22). According to Irenaeus, Paul understands life in the flesh as a fruitful labor because he (like all Christians) is called to manifest Jesus in his very body. He cites a passage from Paul's letter to the Corinthians, where the apostle writes about the trials and difficulties associated with his ministry. In this passage Paul writes that he and all Christians are

> always carrying about in the body the dying of Jesus, so that the life of Jesus may also be manifested in our body. For we who live are constantly being given up to death for the sake of Jesus, so that the life of Jesus may be manifested in our mortal flesh (2 Cor 4:10–11).[23]

According to Irenaeus, we learn from other places in Paul's letter to the Corinthians that "the Spirit is bound with the flesh," such as when he tells the Corinthians they are a "letter of Christ" written not with ink but with the Spirit of the Living God on the "tablets of flesh in your hearts (2 Cor 3:3)." Irenaeus asks, If our hearts of flesh are capable of receiving the Spirit, then "what wonder if at the resurrection they receive the life given by the Spirit?"[24]

Justin Martyr's (100–65) writings against the Gnostics had greatly influenced Irenaeus. Although most of the works that Justin wrote specifically against the Gnostics have been lost, some of his other writings provide us with a window into what his thinking would have been on matters related to the Gnostic controversy. This is true of an essay he wrote on the resurrection, for example. As was mentioned earlier, the Gnostics did not believe in a bodily resurrection. But neither did the Neoplatonists who wrote a great deal about the immortality of the soul. Because Justin viewed the person as a unity of body and soul, he insisted that if the *person* was raised, then both body and soul were raised. As he put it:

> For where He promises to save man, there He gives the promise to the flesh. For what is man but the reasonable animal composed of body and soul? Is the soul by itself man? No; but the soul of man. Would the body be called man? No, but it is called the body of man. If, then, neither of these is by itself man, but that which is made up of the two together is called man, and God has called *man* to life and resurrection, He has called not a part, but the whole, which is the soul and the body. Since would it not be unquestionably absurd, if, while these two are in the same being and according to the same law, the one were saved and the other not?[25]

Recall that Allen Guttmann attributes to Christians a "dualistic ontology" that splits the self into mortal body and immortal soul. As we have seen, in fact, this was a Gnostic and Neoplatonic ontology. And Christian theologians such as Irenaeus and Justin Martyr spent a great deal of time and energy arguing *against* just such an ontology. Indeed, the early Christians were regarded as peculiar by both the Gnostics and Greek philosophers precisely because of their belief that the body, along with the soul, was raised to eternal life.

## THE MANICHEAN CONTROVERSY

The next major doctrinal challenge for Christian theologians dealing with the body came from the Manichean religion, named after its founder Mani, who was born in southern

Mesopotamia in 216 CE. The biographical material about Mani's life describes how, after revelations from his heavenly twin at the age of twelve, he began to question the practices of the Elkesaites, the baptismal sect to which his family belonged. At the age of twenty-four he received his heavenly call to become an "apostle of Light" and eventually attracted a large following. His disciples subsequently traveled the world, preaching in Asia, Africa, and Europe, making Manichaeism a world religion—of which there are still a few living vestiges in our own time. The prominence of his teaching can be seen in the fact that Christians throughout the medieval period continued to describe dualistic heresies, such as those of the Cathars and Waldensians, as Manichean, although it is not always clear that there was direct historical influence.[26]

At the core of the Manichean doctrine was a radical dualism. In an elaborate mythological explanation, Mani described the two eternal principles, Good and Evil, as Light and Darkness, Spirit and Matter, Truth and Error. Originally, there was a first time, or *initium*, when Good and Evil were totally separate, but at some point Darkness tried to take over the kingdom of Light. The struggle of Darkness against Light eventuated in a mingling of the two substances. This is the *middle time*, the present world. The human race is understood to be a mixture of Light and Darkness, with Darkness residing principally in the material world and the body. By ascetical practices, such as abstaining from farming, eating meat, drinking wine, procreation, and fornication, the human person "is enabled to free his true self (which is Light) from Darkness, the body, and matter, and at death return to the Paradise of Light."[27] Through ambassadors of Light, the third time, *finis*, is being prepared in which the total separation of the first time will take place anew.

As with the Gnostics, according to Mani and his followers Christ did not have a real body, experience suffering and death, or rise bodily from the dead. As Augustine put it, "They say that Christ came in recent times to liberate souls, not bodies, and that he did not come in real flesh, but bore a simulated appearance of flesh to deceive human senses. Thus he made a lie, not only of his death, but also of his resurrection."[28]

These doctrines came under attack from many different quarters. The Acts of Archelaus, compiled in 325 CE, is an anti-Manichean *summa* of sorts. Theologians such as John Chrysostom and Vincent of Lerins, along with bishops such as Serapion (Thmuis), Titus (Bostra), Epiphanius (Salamis in Cyprus), Augustine (Hippo), and Caesarius (Arles), all directed their energies toward showing the errors of the Manichean doctrines. As mentioned earlier, dualist teachings continued to appear throughout the medieval period, and later theologians and spiritual writers like Pseudo-Dionysus, John of Damascus, and Thomas Aquinas continued to criticize such views.

Augustine had spent most of his twenties associated with the Manichean sect and was aware of the appeal of their doctrine and very familiar with their teachings and religious practices. He was also widely read in the philosophical literature associated with the classical world and in particular with the Neoplatonism that was flourishing in his day. But it was his conversion to Christianity that led him to consider anew the significance of the material world and the human body in the spiritual life. This happened because in the Christian tradition he was exposed to new sources—which were regarded as revelation—that were very different from the sources of the ancient philosophical world and, in important respects, from those of the Manicheans.

Shortly after his conversion to Christianity, Augustine began to write essays in defense of his new faith against the views of the Manicheans. For Augustine, one of the fundamental problems with the Manichean approach—as had also been true with the Gnostics—was that they denied the validity of Old Testament writings and hence of the account of the creation of the world described in the Book of Genesis. He asks, for example, in *The Morals of the Catholic Church*:

> Will you say that you grant that we are bound to love God, but not the God worshipped by those who acknowledge the authority of the Old Testament? In that case you refuse to worship the God who made heaven and earth, for this is the God set forth through all these books.[29]

The most important thing one learns from the account of creation in Genesis, according to Augustine, is that the created world is very good.

> After each of God's works, is added, "And God saw that it was good," and after the completion of the whole series we have, "And God saw all that he had made, and, behold, it was very good." The meaning of this is that there is only one cause for the creation of the world— the purpose of God's goodness in the creation of good.[30]

Augustine also points out that, according to the Genesis account of creation, the human person was created in the image and likeness of God. This idea would be very important for Augustine's understanding of sin and its effects and the process of redemption.

As theologians who preceded him had, Augustine understood the person to be a unity of body and soul. Since this was the case, he pointed out that the body was integrally involved in the dynamics of the Christian life. As he put it:

> The body is by nature certainly different from the soul, but it is not alien to the nature of human beings. The

soul is not made up of the body, but human beings are made up of soul and body, and surely, whom God sets free, he sets free as a whole person. For this reason the Savior himself assumed a whole human nature, freeing us in the whole he had made.[31]

The last sentence is very important. Augustine's belief in the incarnation had a significant influence on his valuation of the body, as had also been true for Irenaeus and other early Christian theologians. As was mentioned, the Gnostics and Manicheans denied this central Christian belief. But it also confounded the philosophers of the ancient world, including the Neoplatonists of Augustine's day. In the *Confessions*, Augustine writes about being given some books of the Platonists in his younger years. He comments on the many themes in the writings of the Platonists—and these were many—that were analogous to themes in Christian theology. "But I did not find (in these books) that *the Word became flesh*,"[32] he wrote. "These books did not tell me that *He emptied himself, taking the form of a servant, being made in the likeness of men, and in habit found as a man*; or that *He humbled himself becoming obedient unto death, even to the death of the cross....*I did not read (there) that *in due time He died for the ungodly....*"[33]

Similar to Irenaeus, Augustine thought that one of the reasons why Gnostics and Manicheans had developed such negative views about the human body was that they misunderstood what Paul meant when he used the word *flesh*. When Paul wrote, "The flesh profits nothing," Augustine argued, he didn't mean that the human body was of no value.

For if the flesh profits nothing, the Word had not been made flesh that it might dwell in us. If through the flesh Christ has greatly profited us, how does the flesh profit nothing? But it is through the flesh that the spirit acted for our salvation....For how should the sound of the Word reach us except through the voice of the flesh?[34]

Augustine had a different way of interpreting what Paul meant by the term *flesh* than Irenaeus did, however. In his later writings, Augustine turns his attention specifically to Paul's phrases "living by the rule of the flesh" and "living by the rule of the spirit." For Augustine, the term *flesh* in these cases, and in other of Paul's writings, is being used as a synecdoche, or a way of referring to a part to stand for the whole. He quotes a passage from Paul's epistle to the Galatians in which the apostle writes:

> It is obvious what the works of the flesh are: such things as fornication, impurity, lust, sorcery, enmity, quarrelsomeness, jealousy, animosity, dissension, party intrigue, envy, drunkenness, drunken orgies and so on.[35]

Augustine points out that among the "works of the flesh" that Paul says are obvious—and lists and condemns—one finds

> not only those concerned with sensual pleasure, like fornication, impurity, lust, drunkenness and drunken orgies, but also those which show faults of the mind, which have nothing to do with sensual indulgence. For anyone can see that devotion to idols, sorcery, enmity, quarrelsomeness, jealousy, animosity, party intrigue, envy—all these are faults of the mind, not of the body.[36]

According to Augustine, the fact that Paul so clearly writes about the works of the flesh as entailing disorder at the level of the mind is evidence that the term *flesh* in the phrase "the rule of the flesh" is being used to denote the whole person.

Can anyone feel enmity except in the mind?...And by the same token, no one doubts that animosities are concerned with animus, with the mind. It follows that the reason why "the teacher of the Gentiles in faith and truth" gives the name of "works of the flesh" to those and similar failings is simply that he intends the word "flesh" to be taken as meaning "man" by the "part for the whole" figure of speech.[37]

According to Augustine, just as life "by the rule of the flesh" referred to the life of the whole person, body and soul, lived according to human standards, so too life "by the rule of the spirit" referred to the life of the whole person, body and soul, as oriented toward God.

In his writings against the Manicheans, Augustine made use of the doctrine of the Fall to account for the origin of sin and evil in the world. This doctrine allowed him to maintain what was written in Genesis about the goodness of the created world and the human person created in the image and likeness of God and also account for the existence of sin and moral evil in the world. In this account, moral evil exists because of free human choices. The sin of Adam has wounded human beings and made it more difficult for us to use our freedom in the right way. We are able to experience healing and redemption in Christ, however, who offers us "new life." According to Augustine, this was very different from the Manichean view:

They attribute the origin of sins, not to the free choice of the will, but to the substance of the opposing nation which they teach was mingled with human beings. They say that the concupiscence of the flesh, by which the flesh lusts against the spirit, is not a weakness present in us as a result of the nature that was vitiated in the first man. Rather, they insist that it is [a] contrary substance....They say that these two souls, or two minds, one good, the other bad, are in conflict in a single human being, when the flesh lusts against the spirit and the spirit against the flesh. This defect is not, as we say, healed in us as something that will not exist at all.[38]

Augustine is most concerned in this passage to counter the view that evil has a substantial existence in any of the created things of this world. The Manicheans do give evil such a place in the very constitution of the world—especially in the material world and the embodied life of human beings. As Augustine points out, they attribute the origin of sins not to a free choice, but to something in the very makeup or constitution of the human person. They claim that the concupiscence of the flesh is not simply a weakness in human beings, which can be healed, but is due to a human nature that is eternally divided between flesh and spirit.[39]

To counter the view that evil has a substantial existence in the created order of things, Augustine repeatedly insists that "all nature, as nature, is good." In his account, evil could only be understood as a privation, or a lack of what should be there for a created thing to be what it is. Even the privations of natures remind us of the more fundamental goodness of all that has been created. As he put it:

Even the defects bear witness to the goodness of the natures. For what is evil by reason of its defect is good by reason of its nature. A defect is against nature, because it harms a nature, and it would not harm it if it did not lessen its goodness. Therefore, evil is only a privation of good. Thus it never exists except in some good thing....[40]

For Augustine, sin itself was understood as "contrary to nature," that is, to human nature as it was originally created in the image and likeness of God. The effects of original sin defaced the image on God in the human person, and a person's own sins furthered this process. Redemption, however, involved recovery of this image of God in the person. Such an insight would have significant pastoral implications, because it suggested that the process of reconciliation involved both the restoration of right relationship with God and other people *and* of the person to health and wholeness. "An evil is eradicated," he wrote, "…by the healing and restoration of the original which had been corrupted and debased."[41]

The emphasis on the goodness of all creation and the explanation of evil as a privation or lack was common among later Christian writers. In the fifth or sixth century, Pseudo-Dionysus wrote that since everything that has existence is from the Good and is good, evil is "due to a defect rather than to a capacity."[42]

> Whatever is, is from the Good, is good and desires the beautiful and the Good, by desiring to exist, to live and to think. They are called evil because of the deprivation, the abandonment, the rejection of the virtues which are appropriate to them.[43]

Dionysus and other Christian theologians emphasized especially that the material world and the human body were good as they were created by God, because these were the parts of the created world most commonly associated with evil by the Gnostics and Manicheans.

> Surely matter cannot be evil. If it has being in no way at all, then it is neither good nor evil. If it has some kind of being then it must derive from the Good, since every being owes its origin to the Good.…
>
> If it is said that matter is a necessity for the fulfillment of the whole cosmos, how can matter be evil?[44]

## "The Spirit Is Bound with the Flesh"

In the thirteenth century Thomas Aquinas reiterated similar themes when he wrote:

> It is impossible for any being, as a being, to be evil. This is why Genesis (1:31) states: "God saw all the things that He had made, and they were very good"; and Ecclesiastes (3:11): "He hath made all things good in their time"; and also I Timothy (4:4): "Every creature of God is good." And Dionysus, in chapter four of *On the Divine Names*, says that "evil is not an existing thing," that is, in itself; "nor is it something among things that have existence," but it is a sort of accident, something like whiteness or blackness. Through this consideration, the error of the Manicheans is refuted, for they claimed that some things are evil in their very natures.[45]

Thomas insisted, as earlier theologians had, that the human person was a unity of body and soul. His approach was new, however, in that he followed Aristotle in understanding the soul as the form of the body. For Thomas, the soul is the first principle of life in all living things, which is what gives them their essential characteristics or features.[46]

According to Thomas, human beings are creatures of flesh and blood. This is what it means to say that they are "rational *animals*." Brian Davies explains:

> They are, for instance, capable of physical movement. And they have biological characteristics. They have the capacity to grow and reproduce. They have the need and capacity to eat. These characteristics are not, for Aquinas, optional extras which people can take up and discard. They are essential elements in the make-up of a human being. And they are very much bound up with what is physical or material.[47]

In other words, the body is a constitutive dimension of the human person, or as Thomas puts it, "It belongs to the very conception of 'human being' that there be soul, flesh and bone."[48]

According to Thomas, because human beings are a unity of body and soul, it is impossible for a person to understand anything except by turning to the material world and to sense images. As he puts it, "Human minds, existing in bodies, know first the natures of material things, and by knowing the natures of what they see derive some knowledge of what they cannot see."[49] In the sacraments, then, God is simply dealing with Christians in a manner that corresponds to the unity of human nature, leading them "by way of the physical world" to an understanding of spiritual truths. By the "bodily exercises" that are the sacraments, the Christian is trained to avoid superstitious practices, and all manner of harmful action associated with sin, thereby being preserved from "bodily hurt."[50]

# THE ICONOCLASTIC CONTROVERSY

As was mentioned in chapter 1, the controversy surrounding the use of images in Christian worship, which came to the fore in the eighth century, hinged on different understandings of the place of the material world and the human body in the Christian life. John of Damascus was one of the most important theologians who argued for the appropriateness of the use of images in Christian worship. Just as Irenaeus and Augustine had done before him, John repeatedly refers his opponents to the Genesis account of creation to emphasize the goodness of the material world. "You despise matter, and call it contemptible," he wrote to his opponents. "So did the Manicheans, but the divine Scriptures proclaim it good, for it says, 'And God saw everything that he had made, and behold, it was very good.' Therefore I declare that matter is the creation of God, and a good thing."[51] Since this is the case, John writes that it is appropriate to make use of objects from the material world in worship. And he provides many examples of the Israelites being commanded by God to make and then use material objects, such as the jar of manna, Aaron's staff, cherubim, the ark, the meeting tent, acacia wood, oil for the light, and so on, in their worship.

Those who argued against the use of images in Christian worship appealed to the Old Testament insistence on worshiping God alone and not making graven images. With regard to depicting God himself, John of Damascus concurred that the prohibition was appropriate during earlier times, because it made no sense to attempt to make an image of the "immeasurable, uncircumscribed, invisible God."[52] But in his view, when the "Word became flesh and dwelt among us," the situation was radically altered.

> It is obvious that when you contemplate God becoming man, then you may depict Him clothed in human form. When the invisible One becomes visible to the flesh, you may then draw His likeness. When He who is bodiless…is found in a body of flesh, then you may draw His image and show it to anyone willing to gaze upon it. Depict His wonderful condescension, His birth from the Virgin, His baptism in the Jordan, His transfiguration on Tabor, His sufferings….Show His saving cross, the tomb, the resurrection, the ascension into the heavens. Use every kind of drawing, word, or color. Fear not; have no anxiety….[53]

In the view of John of Damascus, Jesus is the "precisely similar" image of the invisible God, and he "reveals the Father in His own person."[54] In this sense, worship in the strict sense (what he calls "adoration") is due to him. Representations of Jesus in images, however, are not "precisely similar" to Jesus himself and so are not due worship in the strict sense; rather they are venerated because they remind believers of Jesus through whom their salvation has come. Such images are meant as aids to Christian prayer, and in this sense, have the capacity to help Christians enter into communion with Jesus and his Father in the Spirit.

For John, the belief that the "Word became flesh" should heighten the Christian's appreciation of the goodness and value of the material world. As he put it:

> I salute all…matter with reverence, because God has filled it with his grace and power. Through it my salvation has come to me. Was not the thrice-happy and thrice-blessed wood of the cross matter? Was not the holy and exalted mountain of Calvary matter? What of the life-bearing rock, the holy and life-giving tomb, the fountain of our resurrection, was it not matter? Is not the ink in the most holy Gospel-book matter?… Reverence God and His friends; follow the inspiration of the Holy Spirit. Do not despise matter, for it is not despicable. To think such things is Manichean.[55]

Because John understood the human person to be a unity of body and soul, he argues that the person arrives at knowledge of the truth by turning to the material things of this world. And this is the case even with regard to spiritual matters.

> A certain perception takes place in the brain, prompted by the bodily senses, which is then transmitted to the faculties of discernment, and adds to the treasury of knowledge something that was not there before. The eloquent Gregory says that the mind which is determined to ignore corporeal things will find itself weak-

ened and frustrated. Since the creation of the world the invisible things of God are clearly seen by means of images.[56]

John insisted that it was the whole person, body and soul, who engaged in the various Christian spiritual practices and who experienced healing and new life in Christ by doing so.

The apostles saw the Lord with bodily eyes; others saw the apostles, and others the martyrs. I too desire to see them both spiritually and physically and receive the remedy by which the ills of both soul and body (for I am composed of both) may be healed....You, perhaps, are superior to me, and have risen so far above bodily things that you have become virtually immaterial and feel free to make light of all visible things, but since I am human and clothed with a body, I desire to see and be present with the saints physically. Condescend from your heights to my lowly state of mind....[57]

Once again, it is clear that Sage and Eitzen's claim that Christianity was built on a foundation of asceticism, which is "a belief that evil exists in the body," is actually a description of Gnostic and Manichean positions. Christian theologians were spending a great deal of time and energy arguing *against just this position* in the early church and during the medieval period. They insisted, over against these heresies, that the body was constitutive of human personhood. This was the theological basis for the emergence of religious practices, including the sacraments and use of images in worship, that involved the body so integrally.

# ASCETICISM IN THE CHRISTIAN LIFE

Given Christian attitudes toward the material world and the human body, it should not be surprising to learn that Christian writers tended to view the ascetical life as situated in the context of a good creation and as having a healing effect; at times they criticized approaches to asceticism that were based on a rejection of the material world or the human body per se. John of Chrysostom contrasts the motivation for self-denial of the monks in the desert with that of the Manicheans, for example:

> They (the monks) say, "Glory be to You, O Lord; glory be to You, O Holy One; glory be to You, O King; that You have given us food to make us glad."
>
> Since not for the greater things only, but also for the lesser, we ought to give thanks. And they do give thanks for these also, putting to shame the heresy of the Manicheans, and of as many as affirm our present life to be evil. For lest for their high self-command... you should suspect them of abhorring the meat, like the heretics mentioned, who choke themselves to death; they by their prayer teach you, that not from abhorrence of God's creatures they abstain from most of them, but as exercising self-restraint.[58]

According to Justin Martyr, Christians were motivated to deny themselves and engage in ascetical practices because of their positive regard for the body and hope for its future resurrection. If Christians did not believe in the resurrection of the body, it would make sense for them to imitate physicians who, when they get a patient who is despaired of and incurable, allow him to indulge his desires, because they know that he is dying. Those who "hate the flesh, and cast it out of its inheri-

understanding are examples of intellectual virtues. Prudence is also an intellectual virtue, but one that has a relationship to the moral virtues because it is the virtue of reasoning well about what to do, or how to live one's life. According to Thomas, it is not enough to "know the good" to be a virtuous person. One must also desire the right thing in the right way at the right time. And so the appetites or passions are of fundamental importance in living a virtuous life.

In part because of the effects of original sin, we find it difficult to live virtuously, and our passions are often not in accordance with reason. One of the ways this can be rectified is by practicing the moral virtues of temperance, justice, and fortitude, which provide a kind of schooling for the passions. When our passions incite us to the pursuit of pleasure beyond reason, for example, temperance serves as a "curb." When the passions withdraw us "from following the dictate of reason, e.g., through fear of danger or toil, and then man needs to be strengthened for that which reason dictates, lest he turn back...to this end there is *fortitude*."[65]

But the passions themselves are neither good nor bad. They are simply a part of our humanity. Thomas rejects the Stoic notion that the wise person is the one whom passions never disturb. Neither are the passions themselves maladies, as Cicero had said. For Thomas, problems only arise when the passions are not in accordance with reason. But this is not to condemn the passions themselves. This, after all, would be to condemn the body as well. "To be completely free of passions," as Etienne Gilson has written, "we should have to be without a body, to be something more than just a man."[66] Gilson explains Thomas's position as follows:

> To say that man must pursue truth with his whole soul
> is to say that he must pursue it with his whole body, for

the soul does not know without the body. Similarly, man must pursue good with his whole body, if he wishes to pursue it with his whole soul. To act in any other way, is to pretend to the moral code of angels and thereby run the risk of not attaining even the moral life that belongs to man. Practical wisdom does not exclude the passions but busies itself with regulating, or ordering and using them. The passions of the wise man are an integral part of his moral life.[67]

For Thomas, grace perfects nature in that it helps toward the healing of our nature, which has been wounded by original sin. More specifically, grace helps the person to integrate his passions and appetites into his life in a way that is in accordance with reason. The person participates in this process by making an effort to grow in the virtues. But grace also elevates him to a kind of sharing or participation in the divine life, as the person grows in the theological virtues of faith, hope, and love. These virtues are infused in him, or are a gift of God. In this sense, for Thomas, two kinds of perfection or happiness are proper to the human person. The first is whatever pertains to human nature itself, and the second is the sharing or participation in the divine life, which is possible simply because of the gratuitous gift of God.

> Now man's happiness is twofold....One is proportionate to human nature, a happiness, to wit, which man can obtain by means of his natural principles. The other is a happiness surpassing man's nature, and which man can obtain by the power of God alone, by a kind of participation of the Godhead, about which it is written (2 Pet 1:4) that by Christ we are made partakers of the Divine nature.[68]

# CONCLUSION

Contrary to a recurring narrative in the writing of the history of sport, Christians in the early church and in the medieval period repeatedly insisted on the importance of the material world and the human body in the Christian life over against views held by Gnostics and Manicheans and others. They developed their arguments by appealing to central Christian beliefs regarding the goodness of the created world, the Word becoming flesh and the resurrection of the whole person, body and soul. Such views provided a theological foundation for the use of the material things of this world in the sacraments and the use of images in worship, as well as the many other religious practices that involved the human body so integrally. These views also influenced how Christians thought about asceticism. For Christian theologians, asceticism was not about disengaging from the material world because it was regarded as evil or denying the body because it was always (and only) associated with sin. Rather, the most influential theologians understood ascetical practices to be situated in the context of a good creation and as attempts to "check" inordinate desires for the created things of this world. This was done so that they might experience life as whole persons in a fuller and richer way, and, in the end, risen life with Christ. This more accurate understanding of the views of early and medieval Christians about the material world and the human body helps us to understand how a religious culture could have emerged in which bodily activities such as games and sports were easily accepted. But there were other factors involved as well, which had to do with how Christians understood the relationship between faith and culture, and the place of play in a virtuous life and its relationship to spiritual values. We turn to these topics in the next chapter.

# CHAPTER FOUR

# "I HAVE RUN THE RACE, I HAVE FOUGHT THE FIGHT"

## ST. PAUL AND THE EARLY CHURCH

As we have seen, contrary to a commonly held view among those who write about the history of sport in the West, Christians during the medieval period repeatedly emphasized the importance of the material world and the human body as constitutive of human personhood. These emphases had a profound influence on the religious culture that emerged in the Middle Ages as well as on the development of religious practices such as the sacraments and the use of images in worship. These emphases also help us to understand how bodily activities such as games and sports could have been so easily integrated into the life of medieval Christians, engaged in on Sundays, feast days, and holy days, and depicted in artistic representations in church buildings and prayer books.

Acceptance of games and sports also had to do with attitudes toward culture. One of the most important decisions made by the leaders of the early church was that the Gentiles did not need to undergo circumcision—that is, become Jewish—before they could be baptized as Christians. Theologically, this decision was based on the doctrine of creation—on the teaching that, as St. Paul put it, God created "all nations to inhabit the whole earth" (Acts 17:26). For Paul, just as all people were created by God, so too all people were affected by the sin of

Adam. Most important, *all* who believed were likewise redeemed through faith in Jesus Christ. This theological position was confirmed by the experience of the outpouring of God's grace in the lives of Gentiles, which the leaders of the early church themselves had witnessed. As the author of Acts put it, "The circumcised believers who had come with Peter were astounded that the gift of the Holy Spirit had been poured out even on the Gentiles, for they heard them speaking in tongues and extolling God" (Acts 10:45–46). The decision to accept Gentiles into the Christian community without requiring them to adhere to Jewish law would have a significant influence on future developments in the Christian church. For one thing, it was an important statement about the universality of the salvation that was offered to people in Jesus Christ. The decision also set a precedent—recorded in scripture—for accepting peoples from diverse cultures, along with their traditions and customs, into the Christian community.

One of the more immediate consequences of this decision was that Christian theologians began to think through the various aspects of their faith in dialogue with, and sometimes in opposition to, Greek philosophical thought. This is a well-known phenomenon about which much has been written. But not much has been written about the relationship between Greek athletic culture and early Christian spirituality. This relationship is evident in the writings of the apostle Paul—a Greek-speaking Jew—who used athletic imagery as a matter of course to describe the Christian life in his letters to the Greeks living in places like Corinth and Phillipi.[1]

Corinth was the sponsor and approximate site of the Isthmian games, Panhellenic games that were held every other year. These were intensely competitive games, and the athletes who competed in them put everything they had into winning; for them, coming in second or third place was a devastating failure. They were very disciplined in their training and unwavering in their commitment, persevering when they were tired, injured, or when the contest was in doubt. The first place prize at the Isthmian games was a wreath made of pine leaves or wild celery.[2]

Philosophers in antiquity thought that the dynamics of the virtuous life could be illustrated using these characteristics of athletic contests as metaphors. For these philosophers, the truly wise person was expected to be disciplined, as was the athlete, in the whole of his or her life. As Roman Garrison has pointed out, the ancient philosophers described the struggles involved in overcoming the temptations of pleasure or persevering during times of trial in terms of the *agon* or contest.[3] In describing the dynamics of the Christian life in athletic metaphors, then, Paul was doing something that was common among the philosophers of antiquity.

Paul's writings were similar to those of the philosophers in their emphasis on self-control, which he thought was necessary for both the Christian and the athlete. He writes in a letter to the Corinthians:

> Do you not know that in a race the runners all compete, but only one receives the prize? Run in such a way that you may win it. Athletes exercise self-control in all things; they do it to receive a perishable wreath, but we an imperishable one. So I do not run aimlessly, nor do I box as though beating the air. (1 Cor 9:24–26)

According to Garrison, while Paul at times emphasizes self-control with reference to the sexual appetite (see 1 Cor 7:9), his insistence on the importance of self-control "in all things" suggests that Paul has in mind one of the broader spiritual virtues that ought to characterize the life of the mature Christian. For

Garrison, this kind of self-control is closely related to *autarkia*, the ability to adapt to all circumstances and endure all conditions and be more than a victor.[4]

For Paul, love is the motivation for the practice of self-control, and for his willingness to adapt to different circumstances. Such love is manifested when Paul renounces his own rights and privileges at times. When he is with Christians who are new or not yet strong in their faith, for example, Paul is willing to abstain from eating meat that has been offered to idols, even though he himself does not object to eating such meat. He abstains in such situations so that he does not cause a fellow believer "to fall" (1 Cor 8:13). Indeed, Paul is motivated by love to become "all things to all people." To the Jews, he became as a Jew; to those outside of the law, as one outside the law; to the weak, he became weak, and so on. For Paul, love does not insist on its own way, or seek its own advantage, but rather "bears all things, believes all things, hopes all things, endures all things" (1 Cor 13:7).

As Garrison shows, Paul's writings could be distinguished from those of the philosophers of antiquity in that he compared the victory on the athletic field with the final victory of the resurrection of the body itself. His letter to the Philippians is characteristic:

> This one thing I do: forgetting what lies behind and straining forward to what lies ahead, I press on toward the goal for the prize of the heavenly call of God in Christ Jesus. But our citizenship is in heaven, and it is from there that we are expecting a Savior, the Lord Jesus Christ. He will transform the body of our humiliation that it may be conformed to the body of his glory, by the power that also enables him to make all things subject to himself. (Phil 3:13b–14; 20–21)

Theologians in the early church continued to make regular use of the athletic contest to describe the dynamics of the Christian life.[5] For example, in the earliest surviving sermon we read:

> So then my brothers, let us contend, knowing that the contest is close at hand, and that many make voyages for perishable prizes, but not all are crowned, except those who have toiled hard and contended well. Let us so contend that we may all be crowned. Let us run the straight course, the immortal contest and let many of us sail to it and contend that we may also receive the crown.[6]

For St. Ambrose, the Christian life was like an athletic contest in that the Christian wrestles with his passions and exercises his body with daily trials of virtue so that he may win the victory of resurrection.

> What is the world but a kind of arena of spiritual strife?...The promoter of this contest is Almighty God....The prizes are the fruits of the earth and the lights of heaven—the former for use in this present life, the latter as a token of eternal life.
>
> Man as a wrestler made a late entry into the (cosmic) contest.....He sees that the "whole creation is groaning with birth-pangs, waiting for the redemption." He chastises his body that it may not be his enemy in the combat. He anoints it with the oil of mercy, he exercises it with daily trials of virtue, he smears himself with dust, he runs for the finishing tape, "but not as uncertainly."
>
> He aims his blows, he lunges with his arms, but not into empty space....Fittingly, therefore, did man (for whom the race was prepared) enter the scene last, so that he might be preceded by the creation of heaven which was to be, so to speak, his prize.

But we wrestle not only "against the spiritualities of wickedness in high places" but also "against flesh and blood." (Eph 6:12) We wrestle with satiety, with the very fruits of the earth, with wine…; we wrestle with wild animals, with the fowls of the air. For our flesh, if pampered by these, cannot be brought into subjection. You see how severe our contests are. Thus the earth is man's competition ground, heaven is his gold medal and therefore it was eminently suitable that, as a friend (of God), what was to minister to his needs should precede him (and provide) his rewards as a competitor.[7]

## MARTYRS AND MONKS AS ATHLETES

Historians of sport who characterize early Christians as having disdain for the body (and therefore little regard for games and sport) often point to writings associated with martyrdom or monasticism to make their argument.[8] But it is precisely in these most arduous and challenging forms of the Christian life that the images of the athlete and the athletic contest are used most regularly as an analogue or metaphor. This is evident in the writings associated with the experience of the early Christian martyrs. Ignatius, bishop of Antioch, used such imagery when writing to Polycarp, bishop of Smyrna, during the persecutions of Christians at the beginning of the second century. He exhorts Polycarp, who would eventually experience martyrdom, to "bear the infirmities of all, like a master athlete."[9] After all, he wrote, "it is like a great athlete to take blows and yet win the fight." He encourages Polycarp, "as God's athlete," to be level headed and calm, for the stakes are immortality and eternal life.[10]

Eusebius of Caesarea included an account of the martyrs of Lyon and Vienne in his monumental fourth-century

*Ecclesiastical History.* He points out in the *History* that most authors who write historical narratives write about the exploits of generals and soldiers, trophies won from enemies, and victories in wars. But the historical narrative of the martyrs of Lyon and Vienne is one of "those who order their lives according to God" and "who have been valiant in most peaceful wars for the true peace of the soul...proclaiming for everlasting memory the struggles of the athletes of piety and their valor that tried so much and the trophies won from demons and victories over unseen opponents and crowns placed upon all their heads."[11]

The account of the martyrs of Lyons and Vienne depicts the persecution and suffering of a woman named Blandina and tells how she, "like a noble athlete," renewed her strength in her confession of faith.[12] For the author of this account, it is what Blandina is enduring in her body that makes it fitting to call her an athlete and is most important for understanding her experience as having significance from a Christian perspective. The way she endured the persecution and suffering enabled others to see "through their sister Him who was crucified for them."[13]

> But Blandina was hung on a stake and was offered as food for the wild beasts that were let in. Since she seemed to be hanging in the form of a cross, and by her firmly intoned prayer, she inspired the combatants with great zeal, as they looked on during the contest and with their outward eyes saw through their sister Him who was crucified for them....[14]

According to the author of this account, when none of the wild beasts touched Blandina she was taken down from the stake and put into prison, "being saved for another contest" so that by conquering through more trials she would make the condemnation of the "crooked Serpent" irrevocable. In the end, although small and weak and greatly despised, she had put on the great and invincible athlete Christ, and in many contests had overcome the Adversary and through the conflict had gained the crown of immortality.[15]

The author of this account of the martyrs of Lyon and Vienne is appalled at the lack of respect the Roman executioners showed for the bodies of the Christians who had been put to death. Those who had been strangled in prison were thrown to the dogs. Then their torturers threw out what was left of the bodies to the wild animals and into the fire, guarding "the heads together with the trunks," so that the Christians could not retrieve them. "So the bodies of the martyrs, after being exhibited and exposed in every way for six days, and then burned and turned to ashes, were swept by the wicked into the Rhone River which flowed nearby, in order that not even a trace of them might still appear upon the earth." This was done "so that none should be buried by us." And indeed, according to the author, "our lot was marked by a great grief because we were unable to bury the bodies in the earth. But in every way they watched, as if they would make some great gain if the bodies should not obtain burial."[16]

As has been mentioned, the early Christian belief in the resurrection of the whole person, body and soul, distinguished Christians from other groups of the time. According to the author of this account, those who put Christians to death in Lyon and Vienne treated the dead bodies the way they did precisely to demonstrate that this belief was ludicrous.

And this they did as if able to conquer God and to deprive them of the rebirth, in order as they said, "that they might not even have hope of resurrection, by trusting in which they introduced among us a strange

101

and new religion and, despite terrors, going readily and joyfully to death; now let us see if they will rise again, and if their God is able to help them and snatch them out of our hands."[17]

These primary sources show us that Christians who were martyred in the early church were not operating out of a "dualistic ontology" whereby they regarded the life of the body as unimportant in comparison with the immortal soul it housed, as Allen Guttmann has claimed. Indeed, it was what they were enduring in their *bodies* that made the athletic metaphors they used so apt, *and* that made their experiences so rich in meaning from a Christian perspective. These Christians complained loudly that the executioners were treating the bodies of the dead in such a degrading way. They were most offended by this because of their belief in the resurrection of the body, a belief that put them at odds with the Gnostics and the Greek philosophical tradition, and that their executioners were trying to show was ludicrous.

Early Christian writers compared the martyrs to athletes because they persevered in the face of trial and tribulation and kept their focus on their goal. For these reasons, the martyrs were also held up as examples for other Christians to imitate. Their lives and martyrdom were depicted in paintings that were intended to draw the viewer into the martyr's experience and encourage him or her to be a participant in the contest. As St. Basil, in his sermon on the blessed martyr Barlaam, writes:

> Now, arise, you renowned painters of the champion's brave deeds, who by your exalted art make images of the General. My praise of the crowned champion is dull compared with the wisdom which inspires your brush with its radiant colors....As I look at the detail in your painting of his struggle, I see his hand among

the flames; your image has made his victory even more brilliant for me. Let the demons be enraged, for they are struck down by the goodness of the martyr, which you have depicted. May his hand, burned in the flames of old, again be revealed as victorious. Would that I may be included in this image, and be united with Christ, the Judge of the contest. To Him be glory unto ages of ages. Amen.[18]

The athlete and athletic competition were also common metaphors and analogies used to describe the life of a monk. In the fourth century, John Cassian, one of the most influential spiritual writers for Western monasticism, regularly used such images. In his book *The Institutes*, Cassian quotes St. Paul, who wrote in a letter to Timothy, "He who contends in the games is not crowned unless he has fought lawfully."[19] For Cassian, it is "only by comparison" that one can know what St. Paul wanted to teach Christians by the example of this world's games. And so it was important to understand the games themselves if one wanted to understand the meaning of the comparison. This is why Cassian gave his fellow monks a detailed explanation of the Olympic games, with a special focus on the training of the athletes.

Cassian pointed out that the aspiring Olympians were tested to see whether they deserved to be admitted to the games in the first place. When a man had been thoroughly examined and found to be worthy and to have a good reputation, it was still necessary to find out whether he had demonstrated sufficient skill and had achieved enough success to warrant admitting him to the Olympic games.

If he offers appropriate proof of his skill and his strength, and in contests with his juniors and his peers, has demonstrated both his proficiency and his strength as a young man; and if he has gone beyond boyish contests and, with his strength now honed by lengthy practice, has, after the presider's trial, received permission to join those who have been approved; and if by his unremitting efforts he has not only shown that he is their equal in strength but has also frequently obtained the palm of victory from among them—only then will he deserve to participate in the noble contests, in which the right to compete is given to none but victors alone and those who have been adorned with the tributes of numerous crowns.[20]

"If we have grasped the example taken from fleshly combat," Cassian wrote, "we ought also, by comparisons with it, to understand the discipline and the order of the spiritual contest."[21] For Cassian, one of the most basic comparisons was that the person who wanted to engage in the "Olympic struggles with vice" that were characteristic of the monastic life must have already shown himself to have lived a life of discipline and training and to have been successful in the struggles against the lesser vices. If he had done so, he would be ready for the more advanced contests.

And when the examination of him who presides over the contest has found us unbesmirched by the notoriety of any base lust, and he has not judged us to be slaves of the flesh, ignoble and unworthy of the Olympic struggles with vice, then we shall be able to do battle against our peers—that is, against the desires and movements of the flesh and the disturbances of the soul. For it is impossible for a full stomach to undertake the struggles of the inner man, nor is it right for someone to be made trial of by more violent battles if he can be overcome in a less important conflict.[22]

When the monk was more advanced, the contest would become more challenging, involving struggles against such vices as pride. For Cassian, "the athlete of Christ, who is lawfully engaged in the spiritual contest and desires to be crowned by the Lord, must also and in every respect strive to destroy this most savage beast (pride), since it devours all the virtues."[23]

Cassian uses the metaphor of the athlete to describe St. Paul himself, who he says is a model for Christians to follow.[24] For Cassian, both the athlete and St. Paul were unwavering in pursuit of their respective goals, victory in the contest and heaven. The attainment of these goals required the chastisement of the flesh. Those who imitated St. Paul, the true athlete, in his strenuous race would also obtain victory in the contest and be crowned with immortality.

> And because he [Paul] knew that he had run tirelessly and with swift and devoted mind "after the fragrance of the ointments" of Christ, and that by chastising his flesh he had won the contest and the spiritual struggle, he confidently adds these words: "Now, a crown of righteousness has been set aside for me, which the Lord, the just judge, will bestow on me that day." And, in order to open to us as well a similar hope of reward, if we should wish to imitate him in his strenuous race, he added: "But not only on me but on all who love his coming." Thus he declares that we shall have a part in his crown on the day of judgment if we love the coming of Christ—not only when he will appear even to the unwilling but also as he daily visits holy souls—and if we obtain victory in the contest by chastising our bodies.[25]

According to Cassian, the ascetical practices of the monastic life were not an end in themselves, so there could be reasons for taking a break from them from time to time. One reason for such a break was to care for the body itself. "If someone refuses to relax a rigorous abstinence when fleshly weakness and frailty demand that he recruit his strength by taking some food, should he not be considered the cruel murderer of his own body rather than the procurer of his salvation?"[26] The liturgical calendar, with its feast days and celebrations, also afforded opportunities to relax the rigors of the ascetic life. "Likewise, when a time of celebration permits the pleasant glow that comes from eating and a meal that is necessarily abundant, if someone wishes to hold to a rigid and unbroken fast, he will certainly be seen not as devout but as confused and irrational."[27] For Cassian, the end of all of the asceticism of monastic life was "that thereby we might be able to attain to love."[28] Indeed, in his view, one of the most important reasons for relaxing asceticism had to do with the need to welcome with love a guest at the monastery, in whom one was to see and reverence Christ.

# RAISE UP AN ATHLETE FOR CHRIST!

The images of the athlete and the athletic contest were not only used with reference to the martyrs and monks, but also with respect to the living of the Christian life in general. John Chrysostom (347–407), bishop of Constantinople, in an address about "The Right Way for Parents to Bring up Their Children," exhorted parents to remember that "we are raising an athlete, let us concentrate our thought on that."[29]

> Raise up an athlete for Christ! I do not mean by this, hold him back from wedlock and send him to desert regions and prepare him to assume the monastic life. It is not this that I mean. I wish for this and used to pray that all might embrace it; but as it seems to be too

heavy a burden, I do not insist upon it. Raise up an athlete for Christ, and teach him that he is living in the world to be reverent from his earliest youth.[30]

For Chrysostom, a young boy could learn valuable lessons by wrestling with members of his own household about the importance of controlling his passions.

And let there be many on all sides to spur the boy on, so that he may be exercised and practiced in controlling his passions among the members of his household. And, just as athletes in the wrestling school train with their friends before the contest, so that when they have succeeded against these they may be invincible against their opponents, even so the boy must be trained at home....Let someone in wrestling stand up to him and defend himself so that the boy may try his strength against him. So, too, let the slaves provoke him often rightly or wrongly, so that he may learn on every occasion to control his passion. If his father provoke him, it is no great test; for the name of father...does not permit him to rebel. But let his companions in age, whether slave or free, do this, that he may learn equability amongst them.[31]

"We shall be able to please God by rearing such athletes for Him," he wrote, "that we and our children may light on the blessings that are promised to them that love Him...."[32]

# THEOLOGIES OF PLAY AND SPORT

When Christians moved from being the persecuted minority into a position of influence in medieval Europe, theologians began thinking about the proper place of play and sport in society. Hugh of St. Victor (d. 1142) was one theologian who did so in his book *The Didascalicon*, which he wrote in Paris in the 1120s. Hugh's book appeared at a time when education centers had moved from the mainly rural monasteries to the cathedral schools of the newly emerging cities. In this different context there was a need for a new overview of the subjects that should be studied and the manner in which they should be taken up. Hugh of St. Victor's book provided just such an overview.[33]

The course of studies described by Hugh was ambitious, given that, in his view, philosophy deals not only with the nature of the things of the created world and the regulation of morals, but with "the theoretical consideration of all human acts."[34] All human acts would have included the enjoyable activities people engaged in for recreation and entertainment. And so the "science of entertainments" was included in the curriculum of the newly emerging cathedral schools as one of the mechanical arts.[35] He also calls this science "theatrics" because the theater was the most popular place for such entertainments in the ancient world. But it was not the only place.

> Some entertainments took place in theatres, some in the entrance porch of buildings, some in gymnasia, some in amphitheaters, some in arenas, some at feasts, some at shrines. In the theater, epics were presented either by recitals or by acting out dramatic roles or using masks or puppets; they held choral processions and dance in the porches. In the gymnasia they wrestled; in the amphitheatres they raced on foot or on horses or in chariots; in the arenas boxers performed; at banquets they made music with songs and instruments and chants, and they played at dice; in the temples at solemn seasons they sang the praises of the gods.[36]

Hugh points out that the ancients reflected upon these activities and gave an explanation of their human and social significance.

> Moreover, they numbered these entertainments among legitimate activities because by temperate motion natural heat is stimulated in the body and by enjoyment the mind is refreshed; or, as is more likely, seeing that people necessarily gathered together for occasional amusement, they desired that places for such amusement might be established to forestall the people's coming together at public houses, where they might commit lewd or criminal acts.[37]

The significance of Hugh's treatment of "entertainments" is primarily in his insistence that they have a legitimate place in society and therefore also among the arts to be studied. His arguing for their inclusion in educational curricula is important because of the level of influence his work would have on education throughout medieval Europe.[38]

An even more extensive consideration of our topic is found in the work of the Dominican theologian, Thomas Aquinas (1225–74). Thomas was writing from the classrooms of the University of Paris, where he was a professor of theology. The emergence of the universities was part and parcel of the even more emphatic development of life in the cities throughout Europe during the thirteenth century. The new mendicant orders, the Dominicans and the Franciscans, had been founded during this time and were to be different from the monastic orders in the extent to which they would go out into the cities among the people and try to relate the gospel message to the realities of everyday life.

Thomas addressed our topic by asking the question in his *Summa Theologica* "Whether there can be a virtue about games (*ludi*)?"[39] For Thomas, as for Aristotle before him, virtue consisted in moderation. And in his view, a moderate person should not be spending the whole of his or her life working or worrying about work. As he puts it:

> *I pray, spare thyself at times: for it becomes a wise person sometimes to relax the high pressure of his attention to work. (Augustine)* Now this relaxation of the mind from work consists in playful words and deeds. Therefore it becomes a wise and virtuous person to have recourse to such things at times. Moreover, the Philosopher assigns to games the virtue of eutrapelia, which we may call *pleasantness.*[40]

For Thomas, while play does relax the high pressure associated with work, playful actions do not have their significance from the point of view of work; he does not view them as the "pause that refreshes" so that laborers can return to their work and be more productive. Rather, playful activities are done for their own sake. As we will see later, this is one of the reasons that play is similar to contemplation in Thomas's view.[41]

According to Thomas, virtue is a matter of living according to the rule of reason. It is possible to sin, then, if one's play exceeds or is less than what is reasonable for a human life. Play can exceed the rule of reason if the very species of the acts employed for fun are discourteous, insolent, scandalous, or obscene.[42] A person's play exceeds the rule of reason, then, if he employs indecent words or deeds or such that cause injury to his neighbor. For Thomas, a person's play can also exceed the rule of reason if there is a lack of concern for circumstances, as when a person makes use of fun "at undue times or places, or out of keeping with the matter in hand, or persons."[43]

In Thomas's view, *it is also possible to sin by having less play in one's life than is reasonable*. A person who is always grave or serious and does not participate in any activities that provide enjoyment would be sinning, according to Thomas.

> In human affairs whatever is against reason is a sin. Now it is against reason for a person to be burdensome to others, by offering no pleasure to others, and by hindering their enjoyment. Wherefore Seneca says "Let your conduct be guided by wisdom so that no one will think you rude, or despise you as a cad."[44]

Sin associated with play would be venial or mortal depending on the effect it had on a person's relationship with God.

Thomas uses these principles when considering whether it is morally acceptable for a person to take up the occupation of play-actor. For Thomas, because "play is necessary for the intercourse of human life" the occupation of play-actor is also lawful. Whatever is useful for human intercourse, after all, may have a lawful employment ascribed to it.

> Wherefore the occupation of play-actors, the object of which is to cheer the heart of man, is not unlawful in itself; nor are they in a state of sin provided that their playing be moderated, namely that they use no unlawful words or deeds in order to amuse, and that they do not introduce play into undue matters and seasons.[45]

With regard to the concern about professional actors spending too much of their time in playful pursuits, Thomas points out that their occupations do not constitute the whole of their lives.

> Although in human affairs, they have no other occupation in reference to other men, nevertheless in reference to themselves, and to God, they perform other actions both serious and virtuous, such as prayer and

the moderation of their own passions and operations, while sometimes they give alms to the poor.[46]

In other writings Thomas points out that play is very similar to contemplation, which he considers the most exalted activity in the Christian life. For him, the two activities are similar because they both are enjoyable and done for their own sake:

There are two features of play which make it appropriate to compare the contemplation of wisdom to playing. First, we enjoy playing, and there is the greatest enjoyment of all to be had in the contemplation of wisdom. As Wisdom says in Ecclesiasticus 24:27, "My spirit is sweeter than honey."

Secondly, playing has no purpose beyond itself; what we do in play is done for its own sake. And the same applies to the pleasures of wisdom. If we are enjoying thinking about the things we long for or the things we are proposing to do, this kind of enjoyment looks beyond itself to something else which we are eager to attain, and if we fail to attain it or if there is a delay in attaining it, our pleasure is mingled with a proportionate distress. As it says in Proverbs 14:13, "Laughter will be mixed with grief." But the contemplation of wisdom contains within itself the cause of its own enjoyment, and so it is not exposed to the kind of anxiety that goes with waiting for something which we lack. This is why it says in Wisdom 8:16, "Her company is without bitterness" (the company of wisdom, that is) "and there is no boredom in living with her." It is for this reason that divine Wisdom compares her enjoyment to playing in Proverbs 8:30, "I enjoyed myself every single day, playing before him...."[47]

In a commentary on a text from Ecclesiasticus, Thomas even refers to contemplation itself as play. The text from Ecclesiasticus he is commenting on reads, "Run ahead into your house and gather yourself there and play there and pursue your thoughts."[48] In contemplation, Thomas writes "it is…necessary that we ourselves should be fully present there, concentrating in such a way that our aim is not diverted to other matters."

> Accordingly the text goes on, "And gather yourself there," that is, draw together your whole intention. And when our interior house is entirely emptied like this and we are fully present there in our intention, the text tells us what we should do: "And play there."[49]

In the fifteenth century, the German humanist Cardinal Nicholas of Cusa wrote about the human and cultural significance of play and its relationship to the spiritual life in his book *De Ludo Globi* or *The Game of Spheres*. Nicholas was an important reformer of the church both in his native Germany and in Rome, where he lived in his later years at the invitation of his close friend Pope Pius II. The setting for *The Game of Spheres* is that Nicholas has just returned from playing a new ball game and engages in dialogues with John and Albert, dukes of Bavaria. These dialogues were about such topics as the creation of the world, the powers of the soul, the origin of various aspects of culture and the dynamics of the Christian life. Nicholas makes use of the ball game itself as the starting point for his reflection on these weighty topics. In his view, it is appropriate to do so, for, as he puts it, "No honest game is entirely lacking in the capacity to instruct. I think that this delightful exercise with the ball represents a significant philosophy for us."[50]

For Nicholas, the capacity that human beings have for inventing new things, such as this ball game, tells us something important about human nature. He tells his interlocutor to notice carefully the ball used in the game; someone skilled at working with wood crafted it in such a way that it would turn in a manner suited to this particular game. Only an intelligent creature could have done this, he points out. "For no beast produces a ball and directs its motion to an end," he writes. "Therefore you see that these works of man originate from a power which surpasses that of the other animals of this world."[51]

Intelligence is the power of the human soul that surpasses that of other animals, according to Nicholas. He gives an example to illustrate this point.

> I thought to invent a game of knowledge. I considered how it should be done. Next I decided to make it as you see. Cogitation, consideration, and determination are powers of our souls. No beast has such a thought of inventing a new game which is why the beast does not consider or determine anything about it. These are powers of living reason called the soul and they are alive because they cannot exist without the motion of the living soul.[52]

John questions Nicholas about whether or not animals have the capacity for reason:

> You seem to have said with certainty that the cogitation, consideration, and determination of this game is not in animals. At the same time you don't deny that animals, in making nests, in hunts, and other things we know, think, consider, and determine. How therefore would you prove that these animals are not rational?[53]

Nicholas grants John that activities animals engage in such as hunting and making nests are not irrational but says that these animals are moved by a law that is written into their very natures to do the things they do. "The beast himself is not moved by the induction of reason, which he does not know, but by the necessitating command of nature."

> For this reason we see every member of each species to be compelled and moved in one specific motion, given, as it were, by the law of nature. Our regal and imperial spirit is not bound by this structure. Otherwise we would not invent anything, but would follow only the impetus of nature.[54]

According to Nicholas, "because they lack the free power that is in us," other animals are different from human beings.

> When I invented this game, I thought, I considered, and I determined that which no one else thought, considered or determined, because each person is free to think whatever he wishes. This is why everybody does not think the same thing, because each person has his own free spirit. But beasts do not have this freedom. Therefore they are impelled to [do] those things that they do by their nature so that all the members of each species hunt and make nests the same way.[55]

For Nicholas, the intelligence and freedom that are powers of the human soul and that give human beings the capacity for invention are significant for the development of all aspects of culture:

> For the mind, having the ability of freely conceiving, finds within itself the art of unfolding its conceptions, which now may be called the mastery of inventing. The potters, sculptors, painters, turners, metalworkers, weavers and similar artisans all possess this art. Thus it is that the potter wishes to express and make visibly manifest the pots, dishes, pitchers and other things

that he conceives in his mind so that he will be known as a master.[56]

According to Nicholas, it is human intelligence and freedom that enable human beings to invent new games and sports and that also give rise to the various aspects of culture mentioned earlier. Obviously, they are also the capacities required for intellectual pursuits in the various academic disciplines, including philosophy and theology.

# CONCLUSION

The earliest Christian theologians and spiritual writers, following St. Paul, commonly used the image of the athlete and the athletic contest as analogies and metaphors to describe the dynamics of the Christian life. And they used this imagery most often precisely when the Christian life was most rigorous and demanding, in writings about martyrdom and the monastic vocation. They also used it on occasion when writing about the Christian life in general terms.

When Christians moved to a position of influence in European society, they began to think about the proper place of play and sport in the Christian life. In the twelfth century, Hugh of St. Victor recognized the validity of such activities in society and included their study in the curriculum of the newly emerging cathedral schools. Thomas Aquinas asked in his *Summa Theologica*, "Whether there can be a virtue about games?," and answered in the affirmative. For him, it was immoderate to be working all the time. And so play was necessary for a virtuous life. Indeed, in his view, *it was possible to sin by having too little play in one's life*. Thomas points out that play and contemplation are similar because both are enjoyable and done for their own sake. He even describes contemplation itself as play. For Nicholas of Cusa, human beings are able to invent games and sports because of two powers of the soul, intelligence and freedom. Indeed, for him these two powers are the wellspring for all invention and creativity that is characteristic of human cultures. For Nicholas, this means that games and sports and all the various domains of culture have a close relationship to the spiritual dimension of life.

# CHAPTER FIVE

# "ORDINARY PEOPLE, JUST FRANKLY ENJOYING THEMSELVES LIKE HUMAN BEINGS"

## CATHOLIC TRADITIONS

When one takes the history of Catholic theology and spirituality seriously, the relationship between Catholicism and play and sport in the West reads very differently from the dominant narrative articulated by sport historians and other scholars. It was not only recently, and reluctantly, that Catholics began to participate in or pay attention to sports. Rather, they were playing games and sports for several centuries before they arrived in the New World. The view that the material world was good and that the human person was a unity of body and soul was part of what led Catholics to accept play and sport. So too was the tendency to incorporate elements of the cultures of the people who became Christian into the life of the faith community. The reason that play and games could be a part of a virtuous life had to do with the Aristotelian emphasis on moderation. In this case, that meant that a person should not be working or worrying about work all the time. A moderate and therefore virtuous life also would include enjoyable activities such as play and sport. According to Thomas Aquinas and Nicholas of Cusa, play was intimately connected to the spiritual dimension of life.

## *Jesuit Schools and Parishes in the United States*

Catholics brought these cultural, theological, and spiritual traditions with them to the early American colonies—at least, to the colonies where they were allowed to live.[1] In the latter part of the eighteenth century, John Carroll, the first Catholic bishop of the United States (in Baltimore), started an academy—to which Georgetown Preparatory School and Georgetown University trace their roots—on which he placed all his "hopes of permanency, & success of our H[oly] Religion in the United States."[2]

Carroll was a former Jesuit. The Society of Jesus had been suppressed in 1773, and Carroll and several other Jesuits in the early colonies were left without a religious community with which to be affiliated. These former Jesuits continued the educational traditions of the Society, however, which were well known among former members of the order who were living in Europe and the colonies. And one of these traditions had to do with the incorporation of games and sports into the school curriculum.

The public advertisement for the "College of George-Town" of 1798 states that the college is dedicated to "the improvement of youth in the three important branches of *Physical, Moral,* and *Literary* education." After pointing out that the college is situated on one of the healthiest spots and commands "one of the most delightful prospects in the United States," the advertisement states, "A constant and scrupulous attention to cleanliness, wholesome and regular diet, moderate exercise, and a due proportion of application and relaxation are the means adopted and unwearily pursued, in order to preserve the health of youths, especially those of a tender age."[3] In 1809, the public advertisement points out that "the garden and court adjoining, where the young gentlemen play, are very airy and spacious.

The situation is very pleasant and healthy."[4] And in 1814, the advertisement mentions the same things, along with the comment that "cleanliness, exercise, and whatever contributes to health, are attended to with particular care."[5]

Sports were a part of the rhythm of the school day at Georgetown from the time of its founding, as they had been at the earliest Jesuit schools in Europe. As Joseph Durkin writes:

> Dinner (the midday meal) was followed by "recreation" or playtime for an hour and a half. Spacious playing fields were available. The popular sports were handball, a rudimentary kind of football that was probably more like present-day soccer, and gymnastic exercises. Fencing and boxing also had their devotees....That a sense of irony was not lacking in the Jesuit author of the Rule (that governed life in the academy) is hinted by the admonition that during time of recreation the study hall was locked and no one was allowed to have a book.[6]

Based on what was mentioned earlier about the importance of moderation in one's studies for Ignatius and the early Jesuits, clearly the admonition was meant to be taken seriously.

To accommodate the large numbers of Catholics arriving in the United States in the middle and latter part of the nineteenth century, the Jesuits started colleges in many different regions of the country. These colleges had extensive playgrounds for the students and incorporated ample time for recreation. The 1857–1858 Catalogue of St. Joseph's College in Bardstown, Kentucky, is typical. "The situation is healthy and beautiful: the buildings are spacious and commodious; the refectories and dormitories are large and well ventilated. The play-grounds are extensive and handsomely set with trees." In the "Collegiate Regulations," one reads that "each division has its own playground, Study-Hall, Dormitory and Refectory" and that "every Thursday of the Academic year is a general recreation-day."[7] The 1878–1879 Catalogue of Santa Clara College is more descriptive and reads under the heading "Play-grounds":

> These occupy nearly four acres of ground, gently sloping and sandy, so that very soon after the heaviest rain, they are dry enough for recreation. On three sides are numerous shade trees and seats. Verandas of aggregate length of a thousand feet extend along the building, affording shelter and exercise in rainy weather. There are besides two large gymnasiums and play-rooms supplied with chess and checker games, &c. Athletic games, however, receive more encouragement than others. On Thursday and Sunday those who wish, may go out walking in the country in company with some of the Fathers.[8]

Under the heading "Swimming and Bathing," one reads:

> At the proper season the students are allowed to bathe in an artificial swimming pond 160 feet long and 120 feet wide, located on the school property near the old Mission orchard....Its bottom is sloping so that a part of it is shallow for beginners, while the rest is deep enough for proficient swimmers. The water is supplied by an artesian well in the centre of the pond. To guard against the possibility of accidents, the students are not allowed to go swimming, unless accompanied by some of the tutors. In winter they have warm baths at the College.[9]

A physician also made daily visits to the college.

As Catholics had done for centuries, the Jesuits provided time for recreation for their students on the feast days and holy days of the church year. They also provided an extended vacation at Christmas. Judging from an essay in the Georgetown *College Journal* by Charles de Courcey in 1877, some students were aware of the history of Catholic practices in this regard, as well as some of the rationale on the part of the church for accepting games and recreation. De Courcey points out that some customs, such as games and recreation, of the Saxons and others who became Christian were allowed to continue after their conversion.

> The more harmless customs observed by the Pagans at their festivals of the season were preserved, at least in part, under the Christian regime, not to deprive the self-denying converts of all their former enjoyments, or demand too much of human nature. The Church, ever mindful of the wants of her children, has always acted in this considerate manner towards newly-converted populations.[10]

De Courcey writes about the continuation of earlier cultural traditions at Georgetown, referring specifically to the role of the Lord of Misrule in John Stow's *Survey of London*:

> The Lord of Misrule, corresponding to our master of ceremonies, directed the revels. According to Stow, there was one in the king's palace, one presided in the castle of each nobleman, and the Mayor and Sheriffs of London had their own. A similar officer, the *Praefectus Ludorum*, superintended the Latin plays in the universities. In his inauguration speech, the Lord of Misrule explained to the company that he absolved them of all their wisdom, and they were to be just wise enough to make fools of themselves. After swearing fealty to the merry ruler, the reign of fun and folly was entered upon.[11]

Perhaps the ease with which the Jesuits incorporated physical recreation into the school curriculum should not be surprising, given that the Jesuits themselves played games and sports during their own training, as they had for over two centuries in Europe. Judging from what is written in the "Directions for Novitiate" of the California Province in the late nineteenth century, the men of the California Province viewed games and sports simply as a natural part of the life of a Jesuit novice. Under the heading of "Games" is written:

> Avoid all disputing. Contested points are to be settled by the Captains of the teams with the umpire; at the same time all should show their charity by doing their bit in putting enthusiasm into the game. Nick-names and expressions contrary to charity and brotherly respect must not be had. Morning ball-games must not go beyond 11:20.[12]

There is evidence that some Jesuits did not abandon their love for games and sports just because they had been ordained priests. An 1872 alumnus of Georgetown College, for example, wrote to the *College Journal* about the game of handball at the college in his day:

> This brief and imperfect sketch would be incomplete without some reference to Father Bahan, who was a brilliant and skillful exponent of the game. Though First Prefect on the small boys' side, he would cross to the other and battle with those of larger growth; and being long of arm and agile of foot, he could strike or kick the ball as occasion required. His agreeable, genial nature endeared him to all.[13]

As had been the case from the earliest days of the Society, most of the new colleges had a "villa" or vacation house owned by the Jesuits to which students could walk for recreation. The 1861–1862 Prospectus for St. Louis University states, for example, "The College Villa, situated near the city, is large and beautiful, with ample buildings, spacious groves, and recreation grounds. Here the students may spend their weekly holiday and the summer vacation in a manner conducive alike to health and relaxation."[14]

The first sporting activities described in any sort of detail in the publications of the Colleges are the "Field Day" games, which took place on special days of the school year. At Santa Clara University, for some years they took place on St. Robert's Day in honor of the university president, Fr. Robert E. Kenna, SJ. The program for the day at Santa Clara in 1875 is entitled, aptly, "Athletic and Humorous Games." These "Field Days" included the usual track and field events, but also sack races, three-legged races, barrel races, greased pig races, and the half-hour "go as you please." Judging from the student descriptions in the college journals, these days were meant to be fun and entertaining—and they attained their purpose.

An unidentified student author at Georgetown, for example, describes the Field Day in 1885 in the *College Journal*. The barrel race, he writes, "was a source of great merriment to the spectators, and of great labor to the participants in the race."

> The contestants were blindfolded and given a barrel, and, at the word "Go," each man seized his barrel, and, after turning around three times, started for the finishing point—at least, where he supposed it to be.
>
> Some, delinquent in their arithmetic, turned but twice and a half; others more than three times, and very few of the twenty starters succeeded in stopping at the right place. The consequence was that the majority, instead of starting toward the object of their search (a stake placed in the middle of the field), went in an entirely different direction; one towards the stone wall, another the tennis court, another the conserva-

tory, and still another toward the new building; this last, whilst looking for the object of his search, happened to collide with an antique white horse and vehicle; the horse, after considering for a few moments, started off on a bee line up the road....

One who happened to have been led by the fragrant odor from the conservatory in the direction of that building became exhausted, and seating himself placidly upon his barrel, and not thinking who might be within hearing, remarked that it was "**** hot work." This promising and attractive young gentleman was an object of admiration to all visitors who chanced to step out on the porch that day.[15]

The Field Day of 1879 at Georgetown had been just as entertaining, judging again from the student account in the *College Journal*. In his description of the greased pig race, the author tells the reader how the pig they were trying to catch would get stuck among cartwheels and stumps and other objects. "Then, in our efforts to disentangle him, he would suddenly rush at us with a perfect crescendo of squeals, attempting an occasional nib at our calves in a way not altogether conducive to social feeling."

The pig disappeared in the crowd, but soon emerged dragging little Henry Touceda after it at a wondrous rate of speed, so that a grave doubt arose in our minds whether Henry had the pig, or the pig had Henry. But as the prize was awarded to the boy, and as the pig was not even mentioned as second, we can confidently assert that Henry won the race.[16]

When interscholastic athletic competitions began toward the end of the nineteenth century and the beginning of the twentieth, the Jesuit schools joined right in. And, as happened in so many other schools in the United States, the varsity teams generated enthusiasm and loyalty toward the schools from just about everyone associated with them. This was true at both the high schools and the universities. One Jesuit prefect at St. John's College in New York City noted in his diary in 1904 that "from the day the boys returned in Sept. till Commencement Day and after, keen interest is taken in the Varsity Team by every boy in the house from seniors down to tots...by the Faculty and even by the workmen." This prefect urged his successor to make sure the team had adequate equipment, "for there is no doubt that the Varsity team helps along cheerfulness and benefits studies and holds old students and attracts new ones."[17]

And, as they had traditionally been, the sports were intimately connected to religious practices. Christa Klein describes, for example, "the blending of baseball and piety at Fordham," which was "nowhere clearer than during Holy Week" during the years the students remained on campus.

> All day long students alternated between the chapel and the playing field. After mass in the morning they went to their respective division ball fields....Although no other mail was distributed, "baseball letters" concerning intervarsity games were made available. After lunch the teams practiced until "Way of the Cross" at 2 p.m. After Tenebrae they played a ball game.[18]

Cultural traditions associated with play and games also continued in the Catholic parishes. For well over a century the Catholic Mass had been outlawed in the English-speaking world, including the colonies of the New World. Thanks to William Penn and the tolerance of the Quakers, however, Catholics were able to celebrate their first Mass in the colonies (openly, in public) at St. Joseph's Parish in Philadelphia in 1733.

*"Ordinary People, Just Frankly Enjoying Themselves"*

The Jesuit Felix Barbelin became pastor at St. Joseph's after the restoration of the Jesuits in 1814, for a tenure that would last from 1838 to 1869. Barbelin continued the Jesuit traditions of religious drama at the parish and encouraged as many parishioners as possible to be involved in the plays there. He also took the children who were involved in the various sodalities on daylong excursions during which they would play games and sports, sing songs, and generally have a good time.

In a letter to the editor of the *Catholic Herald*, a parishioner named Paul writes about a delightful rural excursion to "Point Pleasant" that members of one sodality took under the care and direction of Barbelin.

> The day was spent in all the sports and convivialities which enliven such excursions. Sweet solitude and calm repose, that day at least, took their flight, and the groves of Point Pleasant resounded with the merry shouts of joyous youth, with music and with song. Where shall I find language sweet enough to describe the unrestrained hilarity and innocent mirth of those dear youth, who compose the "Angel's Sodality"? The sparkling eye, the rosy glow of health, the cherub smiles and merry shouts of that sweet-angel band would have driven care and sadness from any heart. How did I wish that all his friends had been there to see their good Father in the midst of his happy family![19]

The author could not restrain the falling tears ("unmanly tears, perhaps, but still, like rain, they fell") as the events of the day alternated with "the chaunt, the prayer, the hymn of praise." When the devotions were finished, "boisterous joy resumed its throne." At the close of day, the whole company marched "in careless order" to the steamer waiting to take them home. Paul closes his letter with an admiring comment about the "inimitable adaptation of the Fathers of the Society of Jesus, for the moral and religious instruction of youth....May their labours of love be duly appreciated at all times and by all people."[20]

Perhaps Paul knew that "all people" were not inclined to appreciate the Jesuits' presence in the United States in the nineteenth century. Some forty years earlier, shortly after the Society of Jesus had been restored in 1814, John Adams had written to Thomas Jefferson:

> I do not like the Resurrection of the Jesuits....Shall We not have Swarms of them here? In as many shapes and disguises as ever a King of the Gypsies, Bamfield More Carew himself, assumed? In the shape of Printers, Editors, Writers, School masters, etc. If ever any Congregation of Men could merit eternal Perdition on Earth and in Hell,...it is this Company of Loiola. Our System however of Religious Liberty must afford them an Asylum.[21]

Thomas Jefferson was of the same mind as Adams. "I dislike, with you, their restoration," he responded, "because it marks a retrograde step from light towards darkness."[22]

## Playful Catholics as the "Other"

Others with not quite so strong a prejudice as Adams or Jefferson noticed that Catholics had a different attitude about recreation and amusements than did their Protestant counterparts and were appreciative of this difference. As mentioned in chapter 1, the geologist Sir Charles Lyell, visiting from England in 1846, commented on the "work ethic" he observed in New England. From the time he and his fellow travelers landed there, Lyell commented on how every person, whether rich or poor, labored from morning until night, without ever indulging in a holiday. He sometimes thought, he said, that the national motto should be "All work and no play."

In New Orleans, where French Catholic cultural traditions continued, however, Lyell describes witnessing something very different. On the feast of Mardi Gras, or "Fat Tuesday," which is celebrated on the day before Ash Wednesday (the beginning of Lent), Lyell writes about witnessing a grand procession through the streets of New Orleans with almost everyone dressed in an outrageous manner, some on horseback, some playing music, and a jolly fat man dressed as Mardi Gras. All wore masks, and, from various locations in the crowd or the balconies, people were armed with bags of flour that they dumped on anyone who seemed particularly proud of his or her attire. For Lyell, it "was quite a novelty and a refreshing sight to see a whole population giving up their minds for a short season to amusement."[23] Lyell noticed that others, who had come from the north, were looking on the festivities as well. "And we were amused by observing the ludicrous surprise, mixed with contempt, of several unmasked, stiff, grave Anglo-Americans from the north, who were witnessing for the first time what seemed to them so much mummery and tomfoolery." Although many of the Protestant citizens took part in the events, "this rude intrusion struck me as a kind of foreshadowing of coming events, emblematic of the violent shock which the invasion of the Anglo-Americans is about to give to the old *regime* of Louisiana." This invasion had not yet caused too many problems; one of the locals tells Lyell that "in spite of the increase of Protestants, he thought there had been as much 'flour and fun' this year as usual."[24]

The novelist Harold Frederic also provides us with a glimpse into these cultural differences in his popular nineteenth-century novel, *The Damnation of Theron Ware.* Frederic describes how Reverend Ware, a Methodist minister, bored with his church's camp meeting one Sunday, stumbles on a Catholic picnic.

> And here the crowds were,—one massed about an enclosure in which young men were playing at football, another gathered further off in a horse-shoe curve at the end of a baseball diamond....Closer at hand, where a shallow stream rippled along over its black-slate bed, some little boys, with legs bared to the thighs, were paddling about, under the charge of two men clad in long black gowns. There were others of these frocked monitors scattered here and there upon the scene,—pallid, close-shaven, monkish figures, who none the less wore modern hats, and superintended with knowledge the games of the period. Theron remembered that these were the Christian Brothers, the semi-monastic teachers of the Catholic schools.[25]

Theron Ware looked in "amazement and exhilaration" upon the spectacle with the shouts, the playful squeals, the dance music, and their "suggestion of universal merriment." He later bumped into the Irish priest, Fr. Forbes, and commented on how everything he sees "interests me enormously":

> It is a revelation to me to see these thousands of good, decent, ordinary people, just frankly enjoying them-selves like human beings. I suppose that in this whole huge crowd there isn't a single person who will men-tion the subject of his soul to any other person all day long.

The priest agrees that this would be a safe assumption, unless it be by way of a "genial profanity." "There used to be some Clare men who said, 'Hell to my soul!' when they missed at quoits, but I haven't heard it for a long time."[26]

# Vince Lombardi and the Immaculata Mighty Macs

In this section, I write about Vince Lombardi and the women on the Immaculata College basketball teams from the Philadelphia area. The point here is not necessarily to highlight these individuals themselves or to hold them up as ideals or models of virtue. Rather, it is to illustrate how the Catholic heritage has been handed on and has influenced sport in the United States in the twentieth century. One of the first things that one notices from these examples is the centuries-old Catholic tendency to accept games and sports. In each case, there is a very easy and natural relationship between being Catholic and participating in sports that reminds one of the attitudes in the earlier periods we have considered.

Vince Lombardi came from a family of Italian immigrants and grew up in Brooklyn, New York. Like many Italians of his generation, Lombardi and his family took their Catholic faith and the daily practices associated with it very seriously. When he was a boy, Lombardi attended daily Mass with his mother. According to David Maraniss:

> The Trinity of Vince Lombardi's early years was religion, family and sports. They seemed intertwined, as inseparable to him as Father, Son and Holy Ghost. The church was not some distant institution to be visited once a week, but part of the rhythm of everyday life. When his mother baked bread, it was one for the Lombardis, one for the priests, with Vince shuttling down the block between his house and the St. Mark's Rectory delivering food and tendering invitations. Father Daniel McCarthy took Vince and his best friend, Joe Goettisheim, to ball games in Flatbush and Coney Island.[27]

One of the reasons the "trinity" of religion, family, and sports was coherent for young Vince Lombardi was the fact that he played sports at the Catholic schools he attended. He had considered a vocation to the priesthood and chose to attend a diocesan preparatory seminary where he played basketball and baseball. When he later decided he wasn't called to the priesthood, he transferred to St. Francis High School, where he played football and discovered his love for the game. He eventually attended Fordham University, run by the Jesuits, where he was one of the linemen who made up the famous Seven Blocks of Granite.

After graduating from Fordham, Lombardi taught Latin and physics and coached football at St. Cecilia High School in New Jersey for eight years. Later, he returned to Fordham, where he coached football for two years, before beginning his legendary professional coaching career with the Green Bay Packers. The influence of Lombardi's Catholic upbringing and Jesuit education stayed with him throughout his life. Throughout his coaching career he prayed on his knees every morning in front of religious statues, carried a rosary in his pocket, attended daily Mass, and made retreats. He routinely associated with priests and nuns, who were often guests at family dinners, and regularly showed up at Packer games and postgame parties. This led some of his players to joke on game day that it was hard to tell what Lombardi wanted more: to win the game or get to heaven. "He wanted both, of course," Maraniss writes.[28]

According to Maraniss, Lombardi was not a proselytizer, however, and he did not invoke God in his locker room pep talks. As he puts it:

> The currents of sports and spirituality within him converged at a deeper point than mere rhetoric. The

fundamental principles that he used in coaching—
repetition, discipline, clarity, faith, subsuming individ-
ual ego to a larger good—were merely extensions of
the religious ethic he learned from the Jesuits. In that
sense, he made no distinction between the practice of
religion and the sport of football.[29]

At the end of his coaching career, the Jesuits at Fordham
invited Lombardi back to the school to honor him with the
Insignis Medal. This medal was awarded to "Catholic leaders for
extraordinary distinction in the service of God through excellent
performance in their professions." The word *insignis* was taken
from the *Spiritual Exercises*, in which Ignatius used it to refer to
someone whose service of God was particularly ardent and distinguished. Lombardi often referred to the day he received this
award at Fordham as "the finest moment" of his life.[30]

Julie Byrne's study of the women basketball players at
Immaculata College, *O God of Players: The Story of the
Immaculata Mighty Macs*, offers another example of the distinc-
tive aspects of a Catholic approach to sport in the United
States. Byrne points out that the study of religion today is
impoverished by a narrow focus that ignores the everyday lives
of ordinary believers. "Scholars do not habitually analyze nonreligious activities to understand religion," she writes. "We are
not used to watching basketball games to shed light on
Catholicism."[31] Since the 1980s, she points out, scholars have
increasingly turned to popular sources and the lived experiences of lay people to learn about religion outside the walls of
the church building. But they still tend to focus on traditional
religious activities or phenomena, such as household devotions, missionary travels, or sacred artifacts when trying to
understand piety. Such studies shed light on formal religious
practices, "but not the many everyday experiences that over-
laid, surrounded, supported, and challenged formal practice."

It is exactly this isolation of faith from life to which many believers object in the study of religion. For a Muslim is a Muslim not only when she prays five times a day, but also when she shops for groceries. A Methodist is a Methodist not only when he works in a soup kitchen, but also when he takes a cruise vacation. And a Catholic is a Catholic not only when she lights votive candles, but also when she plays basketball.[32]

And the young women at Immaculata did play, indeed. From the 1930s through the 1970s, Immaculata, run by the IHM (Immaculate Heart of Mary) sisters, attracted many of the most talented female basketball players from Catholic high schools in the Philadelphia area. The school's varsity basketball program began in 1939 and already had a recognized strong tradition when they defeated a storied Temple team to win the mythical Philadelphia city championship in 1946. In 1972 the Immaculata team won the first women's national basketball tournament, sponsored by the Association for Intercollegiate Athletics for Women. And they repeated as national champions in 1973 and 1974. From that time forward, Byrne writes, "the Immaculata championship teams and their coach Cathy Rush, have been widely credited with revolutionizing the women's game and breaking early barriers to help make girl's [sic] hoops the wildly popular game it is today."[33]

After describing the way the "Mighty Macs" of Immaculata College won the mythical city championship in 1946, Byrne comments that what might be more amazing to those who hear the story in our own time is "that midcentury Philadelphia Catholic girls were playing basketball in the first place. In 1946, before most women ever heard they could play a sport? Catholic girls, whose church was famous for regulating sexuality and gender roles? In Philadelphia, where Catholic leadership had the reputation of being more Roman than Rome?"[34]

> Catholicism was different from other U.S. faiths because of its populous numbers, diverse composition, institutional strength, separate schools, and antagonism against Protestant Christianity. And perhaps nowhere in the country was Catholic difference more striking than in Philadelphia. The Irish-dominated archdiocese inspired remarks from Catholics and non-Catholics alike for its traditions of authoritarianism, conservatism, insularity and uniformity....
>
> On the other hand, if Philadelphia's Catholic girls, accompanied by busloads of priests, nuns, and family members, were trooping all over the city to play basketball games in gyms full of "publics," perhaps local Catholics did venture outside neighborhood enclaves....If the Philadelphia Catholic school system nurtured the city's best female basketball players, perhaps archdiocesan leadership was more progressive— or less pervasive—than we thought. If girls who played for Catholic schools suffered no censure and indeed got accolades for running, jumping, sweating, fouling, competing, and winning, maybe the faith's vision of femininity allowed for horizons previously invisible.[35]

According to Byrne, from at least the 1920s and 1930s many Catholic girls grew up playing basketball in Philadelphia. They played in their back yards with brothers and sisters and on Catholic grade school teams. They played on the playgrounds and on informal church teams and at recreation centers. When the Catholic Youth Organization (CYO) began in the late 1940s, girls played on parish CYO teams. They tried out for the highly regarded spots on the Catholic high school teams. And the high school girls' teams consistently sold out city venues.

> Catholic league girls did not play for a Philadelphia high school championship, because the public schools did not have squads that could even come close to measuring up. Instead, starting in the forties, crowds of Catholic folk packed Convention Hall for Friday night all-girls double-headers for the entire regular season. As the years went on, tickets for the girls' Catholic League championship, played at the Palestra, and even tickets for big duel matches sold out weeks in advance. "We'd be four thousand girls in that building screaming our heads off," remembered Mary Frank McCormick '50, who played at Convention Hall with her team from Notre Dame Academy....[36]

Byrne points out that nearly all of the 1,800 IHM sisters in the local community in 1951 were from the Philadelphia archdiocese. The IHM sisters who taught at Immaculata, then, "were often city born-and-bred basketball players and fans themselves."[37] The novitiate (house for new members of the community) just across the road from the college had a basketball court for the younger sisters in formation to use during their free time. The sisters filled the stands and buses for almost every game. Sister Mary of Lourdes McDevitt, a former high school basketball star who began her eighteen-year presidency in 1954, often stopped by practices to scrimmage with the girls on the varsity teams.

The sisters also supported the players with prayers. "I would never think of starting a game without praying," said Sister Mary of Lourdes, "not to win but to put them under protection." According to Sister Mary William Hoben, '44, "prayer was very, very essential to whatever we were doing." The basketball players remembered many nuns praying for the team over the years, as well as attending games and cheering for them. "Especially if we were leaving the campus," recalled Barbara Klein Burns '56, "the sisters said, 'Hey, good luck, don't forget we'll pray for you.'...They prayed for your safety to get there...and get back...and then to play a good game. They didn't really care if you won." Byrne points out that when the sisters did attend a game, they had a dramatic presence, filling an entire section of the bleachers in dark blue and white nun's habits. "You could see the sisters in the stands constantly praying for us," said Mary Scharff '77. "You had this really good feeling about everything because it wasn't like we were on our own."[38]

The elderly and infirm nuns who lived on campus at Camilla Hall followed the games closely in their residence. They would set up a radio on the windowsill of the common lounge and gather around in wheelchairs to listen. The sisters in Camilla Hall interjected prayers throughout the game, especially if it seemed that the team was in danger of losing. "If somebody would say, 'They're losing, they're losing!' everybody'd go to the chapel...wheeling their wheelchairs in to pray...for them in the chapel, said Sister Marian William Hoben."[39]

The team members gradually began to appreciate "'the power of so many silent yet boisterous sisters at Camilla,' remembered Lorrie Gable Finelli, '78. 'They helped us so much in all of their prayers,' agreed Mary Scharff, '77. 'They were behind us and supporting us and...we decided...hey, let's support them, too.'"[46] The players began making regular visits to Camilla Hall to see the elderly sisters, and the team even began to hold some of its pep rallies there. What was initially an attempt to give something back to the sisters because of their support grew into something more as these women formed treasured relationships across the generations. Byrne points out that many Mighty Mac players continued to visit the sisters in Camilla Hall long after they had graduated from Immaculata.[40]

According to Byrne, the way the sisters thought about basketball and other sports at their school was rooted in a holistic vision of life inspired by the theology of Thomas Aquinas. The sisters themselves were formed in Thomas's holistic vision during their own theology studies, and they passed it on to their students.

> In other classes and around campus, nuns related subjects and activities back to God, communicating that "all extracurricular activities" were, as former I.C. manager Sister M. Charles Edward Woodward '62 wrote, "an integral part of the wholistic approach to education." Sister Loretta Maria Tenbusch remembered teaching her freshman composition classes that the physical world, including sports, ranked among God's great gifts to humanity. "He has given us all these gifts," she said she always taught, "including the physical, so important, so precious."[41]

Sister Marie Roseanne Bonfini, '57, former president of Immaculata, said that the sisters, building on their community training, taught students that "love of work" should always be complemented with "love of play."[42]

The players themselves echoed similar themes. A 1953 graduate commented that through basketball she came to understand that "religion is in every facet of life," while Dolores Giordano Prokapus, '56, said she viewed basketball as Catholic, because it was "'just part of my life—acknowledging God's presence in all activities.'...'Anything we do with God's help, even playing basketball,' said Patricia Furey McDonnell '53."[43]

# CONCLUSION

Contrary to a common narrative among sport historians, Catholics in the United States did not wait for people with more "enlightened" or secular mind-sets to teach them about acceptance of the body and therefore of games and sport. Nor were they influenced in this regard by Protestant "muscular Christians." Rather, when they arrived in the United States, they simply continued to play games and sports as they had done for many centuries in Europe. The Jesuits, in particular, continued the approach they had taken in Europe for two centuries of including games and sports as part of the daily activities of their students. In the mid- to late nineteenth century, games and sports were meant to provide fun and relaxation for students in the Jesuit schools or young people in the parishes. When the games were played on holy days and Sundays, they alternated easily and naturally with the religious practices on these days. Indeed, Catholics' easy acceptance of games and sports was a part of what made them seem alien and unusual to some in the Protestant majority in the nineteenth and early twentieth centuries.

The approach of Catholics in the United States was influenced by theological traditions as well. The Jesuits and the IHM sisters continued a longer tradition that regarded the human person as a unity of body and soul and that included the body in an integral way in the educational process and in religious practices. They also continued a longer tradition that emphasized that both work and play were important. As we have seen, Thomas Aquinas, the humanists, and early Jesuits thought that there could be a virtue in participating in play and sports because one should not be studying or working all the time. Such a life would be immoderate. The Jesuits continued to give this idea concrete expression in their schools in the United States as they built their schools with playing fields and courtyards and provided ample time for games and sports. The IHM sisters, who studied Thomas Aquinas in their training, emphasized that a "love of work" should be complemented by a "love of play" and encouraged and supported the women basketball players on the school varsity team. Indeed, the young basketball players and the elderly nuns at Camilla Hall formed treasured relationships across the generations, inspired, in part, by their common love of basketball.

# CHAPTER SIX

# "A FORM OF GYMNASTICS OF THE BODY AND OF THE SPIRIT"

The main point of the chapters in this book about lay Catholic involvement in sports (chapters 2 and 5) is that the mainstream Catholic approach, from the medieval period forward, has been one of accepting such activities and incorporating them in the religious cultures and in the educational institutions. The chapters with a theological focus (chapters 1, 3, and 4) showed that this approach was undergirded and supported by several factors, including the Christian understanding of the material world as good and the human person as a unity of body and soul; the view that a virtuous person should be moderate in his studies or work and take time to engage in play and recreation; and an understanding of the relationship between faith and culture, which tended toward the acceptance of non-Christian customs and cultural traditions that were good in themselves (or at least not immoral) and their inclusion in the religious tradition. For some theologians, play itself was even understood to have spiritual significance.

This interpretation is very different from the mainstream interpretations of the history of sport in the West. Most scholars writing about lay Catholic involvement in medieval and early modern European sport tend either to describe the games and sports during these periods and bracket the religious dimension entirely, or to conclude that the religious influence, which fostered a loathing of the flesh, was thoroughly negative with respect to sport. If the latter were true, lay Catholics would have engaged in games and sports in spite of their religious faith rather than because of it.

More needs to be done than simply to show that the mainstream Catholic approach has been accepting of sport, however. We must also ask about the quality of the experiences that people are having in sport in our own context in the United States. The context has changed radically from the medieval and early modern periods, after all. In the case of Vince Lombardi, for example, it appears that sport was very much of a piece with his own Catholic faith. But what about his approach to sport or the value orientations he brought to it? How do these square with a Catholic understanding of the human person and of what is most important in life? It is true that Catholics, and Jesuits in particular, simply joined in with the rest of the schools when interscholastic and intercollegiate athletics began in the late nineteenth and early twentieth centuries. But this was a completely different way for sports to be practiced in educational institutions than anything they had known in the past. And what is one to make of interscholastic or intercollegiate athletics closer to our own time? Intercollegiate athletics, in particular, have become a very significant part of the entertainment industry and media landscape in our country. One only needs to mention the $10.8 billion contract that the National Collegiate Athletic Association (NCAA) recently signed with CBS for televising the men's Division 1 basketball tournament to get a sense of what is happening in this regard. Is it possible for Catholic schools to participate in this system with integrity and in a way that is consistent with their own mission statements? If so, how would that be done?

In a more general sense, elite-level and professional sport have become intimately connected to wealth and status in our society. Sport in medieval or early modern Europe did not have a connection to wealth and status in the same way. How does the connection among sport, wealth, and status in our own context affect sport practices and the persons involved? What are the broader implications in terms of resources in our society and in particular with regard to the situation of the disadvantaged and the poor? Catholic theologians who are reflecting on sport in our contemporary context will need to take seriously the realities of the new context and deal with questions such as these.

# CATHOLIC THEOLOGIANS AND SPORT IN THE CONTEMPORARY CONTEXT

One thing is clear from our long-range study of the Catholic cultural and theological heritage: in some of the core theological principles there is strong support for Catholic theologians to be engaged in reflection on sport as an aspect of culture in the United States. As we have seen, for example, in this tradition there is an insistence on the unity of the human person, body and soul (or body, soul and spirit). Traditionally, the emphasis on the unity of the person has been the rationale for why the body was integrally involved in religious practices, including the sacraments and the use of images in worship. The implication of this understanding of the human person for our own context is that a person who is engaged in a bodily activity such as sport is necessarily impacted in his or her consciousness and even at the level of spirit. As a glance at the daily sports page illustrates, this impact can be for good or ill. When the impact is for the good, the person participating in sport can gain new insights into the meaning of his or her life and his or her relationship to God. Indeed, Pope John Paul II said that the church approves of and encourages sport precisely because it sees it to be "a form of gymnastics of the body and of the spirit."[1] As he put it, "Athletic activity, in fact, highlights not only man's valuable physical abilities, but also his intellectual and spiritual capacities. It is not just physical strength and muscular efficiency, but it also has a soul and must show its complete face."[2]

The church's longer heritage gives Catholic theologians another reason to pay attention to sport in the contemporary context. This has to do with an understanding of the relationship between faith and culture. As has been mentioned, St. Paul was a foundational figure in this regard. As the apostle to the Gentiles, he spent most of his life making the gospel message known to the Greek-speaking world. And his approach involved referencing aspects of the Greek cultural heritage, including sports. He wrote to the citizens of Corinth, as we have seen, "Do you not know that in a race the runners all compete, but only one receives the prize? Run in such a way that you may win it" (1 Cor. 9:24).

Pope John Paul II commented on this passage in a 1984 homily to 80,000 young athletes from around the world at the Olympic Stadium in Rome. He pointed out that Paul, in his attempt to make the gospel known to the Greeks, drew from the concepts, images, terminologies, modes of expression, not only of the Jewish heritage, but also of Hellenic culture. "And he did not hesitate to include sport among the *human values* which he used as points of support and reference for dialogue with the people of his time." According to John Paul II, Paul did not make references to sport merely to illustrate a higher ethical or aesthetic ideal. Rather, Paul recognized the fundamental validity of sport and its role in the formation of the person and of civilizations themselves.

> In this way, St. Paul, continuing the teaching of Jesus, established the Christian attitude towards this as

towards the other expressions of man's natural faculties such as science, learning, work, art, love and social and political commitment. Not an attitude of rejection or flight, but one of respect, esteem, even though correcting and elevating them: in a word, an attitude of *redemption*.[3]

What would an "attitude of redemption" be in relation to sport in our own context, according to John Paul II? It seems that such an attitude starts with an emphasis on the dignity of the human person. Indeed, in John Paul II's view, "the dignity of the human person is the goal and criterion of all sporting activity."[4] For the pope, sport should be practiced in a way that fosters the "freedom and integral development" of the person, which includes his or her spiritual growth. That participation in sport should foster spiritual growth has been a recurring theme in the popes' teachings on sport. Pope John XXIII emphasized this point in an address on "The Educational Value of Sports," saying that "the great value of athletics lies in its particular efficacy for interior perfection."[5] And for Paul VI as well, the practice of sport "facilitates the spiritual well being of man. For sport,—is it not true?—gives self-control and mastery of the instincts, and it prepares for the awakening of the things of the spirit."[6] Most recently, Pope Benedict XVI has pointed out that "through sports, the ecclesial community contributes to the formation of youth, providing a suitable environment for their human and spiritual growth."[7]

## THE PURITAN WORK ETHIC AND PROBLEMS IN YOUTH SPORT

So far this chapter has highlighted how core principles from the Catholic theological tradition provide a rationale for

Catholic theologians to reflect on sport in the contemporary context. However, this topic is unique in that the earlier Catholic cultural and theological traditions with regard to sport were explicitly rejected by the Puritans in the early American colonies and later by most mainstream Protestants in the United States. Since Protestants were so influential in shaping the ethos and value orientations of this country, in later periods most Americans were unaware of this longer heritage or of what was rejected. Because Catholic theologians have not attempted to retrieve this heritage, lay Catholics, who were the bearers of these traditions, have been for the most part unfamiliar with them as well.

But we can learn a great deal about a culture by paying attention to what it rejects. After all, what a culture rejects is intimately related to what it holds most dear. As was mentioned in chapter 1, one reason for the rejection of the feast days and the play and sport associated with them was that the reformers, and especially the Puritans, associated godliness with one's calling or work. And this led to a new level of suspicion of play and a tendency to associate it with sin. Seventeenth-century English Puritan minister Richard Baxter expressed this view in his *Christian Directory*, in which he lamented that his readers

> have no mind of your work, because your mind is so much upon your play....[you] are weary of your business, because your sports withdraw your hearts.... They [play and sports] utterly unfit you, and corrupt your hearts with such a kind of sensual delight, as makes them more backward to all that is good.[8]

The same mentality is articulated in the United States in the nineteenth century by the editors of the Congregationalist magazine *The New Englander*:

## "A Form of Gymnastics of the Body and of the Spirit"

> Let our readers, one and all, remember that we were sent into this world, not for sport and amusement, but for *labor*; not to enjoy and please ourselves, but to serve and glorify God, and be useful to our fellow men. This is the great object and end of life. In pursuing this end, God has indeed permitted us all needful diversion and recreation....But the great end of life after all is *work*.[9] (italics in original)

This heritage has contributed to the work orientation in U.S. culture, and hence to the marginalization of the play element. The effects of this heritage are still felt today. Indeed, even children's sports are often not playful anymore, and many people are taking note of this phenomenon. The *New York Times* recently ran a front-page story about youth sport, for example, in which the author described hearing parents and others telling "tales of overburdened children playing sports out of season, of demands to specialize in a single sport as early as grade school, of competitive pressures that lead to national championships for 9 year olds...."[10] Bruce Ward, the director of physical education and athletics in San Diego's public schools, commented in the article, "The shame of it is you see how hardened these 14-year-olds are by the time they get to high school. They're talented, terrific players, but I don't see the joy. They look tired. They've played so much year-round, they are like little professionals."[11]

When work and productivity in youth sport are overemphasized, the young person can be adversely affected. In the United States today young people who participate in sport suffer from overuse injuries at a dramatically increased rate compared to thirty years ago, for example. In a newspaper interview in 2005, Dr. Lyle Micheli, director of the sports medicine division of Boston Children's Hospital, said that twenty-five years earlier, only 10 percent of the young patients he treated came to him for injuries caused by overuse. But at the time of the interview, he said, such overuse injuries represented 70 percent of the cases he saw.[12] Dr. James Andrews, a nationally prominent sports orthopedist, commented, "You get a kid on the operating table and you say to yourself, 'It's impossible for a 13-year-old to have this kind of wear and tear.' We've got an epidemic going on."[13] Overuse injuries occur so much more often now because parents and coaches are encouraging children to specialize in one sport at younger ages than ever before. These children typically train year-round in one sport, performing the same exercises over and over again. Their bodies aren't mature enough to handle such training, however, and break down. Parents and coaches encourage early specialization so that the young person can gain an edge on others when competing for college athletic scholarships or (if everyone's dreams come true) in elite-level or professional sport. It is easy to see that youth sport is becoming instrumentalized, regarded as a means to ends outside of the activity itself, having to do with money and status.

Of course, in our context, elite-level and professional sport has indeed become connected to a great deal of wealth and status, especially since the mid-twentieth century. This association is in large part owing to the effects of television coverage of sports that began at this time and that has since increased exponentially with the advent of cable television stations that broadcast only sports programming. While this has been very good for the business side of sports, it has also introduced temptations for the athletes themselves. According to former Los Angeles Lakers coach Phil Jackson, when NBA players become seduced by the wealth and fame associated with professional basketball, they end up with swollen egos. This makes it very difficult for them to be good team players or to experience the joy that motivated them to begin playing basketball in the first place. He writes:

> The battle for players' minds begins at an early age. Most talented players start getting special treatment in junior high school, and by the time they reach the pros, they've had eight or more years of being coddled. They have NBA general managers, sporting goods manufacturers, and assorted hucksters dangling money in front of them and an entourage of agents, lawyers, friends, and family members vying for their favor. Then there's the media, which can be the most alluring temptress of all. With so many people telling them how great they are, it's difficult, and, in some cases, impossible, for coaches to get players to check their inflated egos at the gym door.[14]

Jackson's analysis of how professional sports is corrupted resonates with Ignatius of Loyola's understanding of how persons and societies are typically corrupted. In the Two Standards meditation in his *Spiritual Exercises*, Ignatius describes a three-step process in which he says that people can become "ensnared" by coveting riches, which lead to honor and esteem from this world, then to pride. As Ignatius put it:

> People find themselves tempted to covet whatever seems to make them rich, and next because they possess some thing or things they find themselves pursuing and basking in the honor and esteem of this world. Then getting such deference raises up the false sense of personal identity in which a blinding pride has its roots.[15]

According to Ignatius, this "blinding pride" leads to all other vices.

# RESOURCES RELEVANT TO YOUTH SPORT

Some of the theological resources discussed in this book from the earlier Catholic tradition are relevant for the issues facing youth sport today in the United States. The first thing from the earlier heritage that can be helpful is the emphasis on moderation as central to a life of virtue. When Aquinas asks whether there can be a virtue about games, he points out that it behooves a wise person to relax his attention to work. And so, it is virtuous to have play as a part of one's life. Indeed, for him, *it is possible to sin by having too little play in one's life.* Unfortunately, it seems as though this is the situation in youth sport too often today. As Bruce Ward said, many young people appear to be burned out before they even reach high school. They are like little professionals. And the joy is gone. There are probably many factors contributing to this situation. But one of them for many young people is surely the shift from playing for fun to training for a college scholarship or professional contract. As was mentioned earlier, this is what leads many youth to specialize in one sport at a young age, and to overuse injuries.

With respect to the issue of overuse injuries, the humanists have something to teach us today. As we have seen, the humanists also insisted on moderation when considering the *manner and extent to which* young people should engage in sport. They did so by considering the mean in relation to the young person himself. And this involved taking into consideration the characteristics of the young person, including his age, body type, and what was appropriate given his situation in life. Pier Paolo Vergerio, when reflecting on the kinds of physical exercises his students should engage in, wrote that "Age must be taken into account, so that up until the age of puberty they should be subjected to lighter burdens, lest the sinews be worn down, even at this age, or the growth of the body impeded."[16]

We need a focus similar to that of the humanists on the young person and his or her physical and personal development in our time. This is particularly urgent because the health of our young people is being adversely affected by the pursuit of goods external to sport, such as wealth and fame.

## RESOURCES RELEVANT TO ELITE-LEVEL AND PROFESSIONAL SPORTS

The emphasis on moderation as central to a life of virtue is also relevant for elite-level and professional sport. Recall the words of Francois Pierron, from the seventeenth century: "If you love your life," he wrote, "moderate your desires."[17] Indeed, in Pierron's view, "the games which are not moderated by discretion are accompanied and followed by many great misfortunes."[18] Although these words are relevant for youth sport, they are most relevant for what is happening in our time in elite-level and professional sport, where most is at stake in terms of wealth and status. As I write this chapter, the perjury trial for seven-time Cy Young Award winner Roger Clemens is underway. Clemens was recently indicted on charges of obstruction of Congress, perjury, and false statements as a result of testimony he gave to Congress during a 2008 deposition regarding use of performance-enhancing drugs. We have watched a virtual parade of superstar athletes in our time who have fallen on misfortune because they lacked moderation with respect to their desire to win, which manifested itself in the use of performance-enhancing drugs. One thinks of Olympic sprinters Carl Lewis, Marion Jones, and Ben Johnson, who used performance-enhancing drugs to win gold medals and break world records. Unfortunately, the following excerpt from a newspaper article about Tour De France cyclist Floyd Landis is fairly common:

When he won the 2006 Tour de France, Floyd Landis was supposed to be the man who would deliver cycling from its past doping scandals. He was a former Mennonite, a nice guy with a quick wit and a relaxed nature. He was the underdog with a bad hip.

Instead, Landis fell quickly and hard into his own nightmare, which cost him his reputation, his career and more than $2 million.

Landis was stripped of his title more than a year after winning the 2006 Tour when an arbitrator's 2-to-1 decision supported initial findings that Landis had synthetic testosterone in his urine during the race.[19]

The lack of moderation around the desire to win has also led to great misfortune for university athletic programs that violate NCAA rules, sometimes by essentially "buying" high school players. The University of Southern California is only one of the more prominent institutions that has been caught up in this type of scandal in recent years.

Citing major violations by U.S.C.'s football and men's basketball programs, the N.C.A.A. on Thursday barred the Trojans' football program from bowl games in the 2010 and 2011 seasons. U.S.C. will also be forced to vacate all victories in which the Heisman Trophy winner Reggie Bush participated beginning in December 2004—including the Orange Bowl victory that produced the Trojans' Bowl Championship Series title in January 2005—and will be docked 10 scholarships in each of the next three seasons. The harshest penalties stem from improper benefits given to Bush and the basketball player O. J. Mayo, which the N.C.A.A. committee on infractions said struck at the heart of the association's amateurism principle.[20]

Reggie Bush has subsequently returned his Heisman Trophy.

Unfortunately, it is also common for college and professional athletes to find themselves in trouble off the court or playing field in our time. In many cases, alcohol or drug use is involved. One way of understanding this is to consider that these athletes have been so devoted to hard work, productivity, excellence in all spheres that they don't know how to relax or get a break from the pressures. When they are growing up, if school is like work, and sport participation is like work, when do young athletes learn how to relax and enjoy life? What activities provide "recreation and rest" for their souls, as Thomas Aquinas says? I'm afraid the whole orientation of their lives, which is encouraged by teachers and coaches in the educational institutions they attend, moves in a direction that is opposed to moderation. Is it surprising that they don't know what to do for recreation and relaxation, and that they end up overusing alcohol or other drugs and sometimes making poor decisions while doing so?

## PLAY AND SPIRITUAL VALUES

As we have seen, educators and theologians from the earlier historical periods took play itself seriously. Play was regarded as important for a balanced life. At times the humanists and early Jesuits describe its value as enabling students to return to their studies with better concentration. For Thomas Aquinas, however, play does not have its importance in relation to something else. It is not the "pause that refreshes" so that the person can get back to what is *really* important—that is, work—with more energy and vitality. For Thomas, play is significant in itself. Indeed, play is like contemplation, because both activities are enjoyable and done for their own sake.

Catholic liturgical theologian Romano Guardini agrees with Thomas Aquinas that play and contemplation share similarities. Indeed, in Guardini's view, the liturgy itself is a kind of play. For him, the didactic aim of the liturgy is that of teaching the soul "not to see purposes everywhere." In this sense, the liturgy is similar to the play of the child or the life of art: "It has no purpose, but it is full of profound meaning."[21]

> The soul must learn to abandon, at least in prayer, the restlessness of purposeful activity; it must learn to waste time for the sake of God, and to be prepared for the sacred game with sayings and thoughts and gestures, without always immediately asking "why?" and "wherefore?" It must learn not to be continually yearning to do something, to attack something, to accomplish something useful, but to play the divinely ordained game of the liturgy in liberty and beauty and holy joy before God.[22]

An important part of the task of Catholic theologians in the contemporary context is to safeguard the play element in sport, and particularly in youth sport. After all, if play is similar to contemplation, then the experiences of a person at play must themselves be of considerable significance. That is, there is potentially a "through line" from children playing hopscotch or the experience of a fifteen-year-old playing basketball to the experience of contemplation or the prayer of the liturgy. As Peter Berger has put it, "The experience of joyful play is not something that must be sought on some mystical margin of existence. It can be readily found in the reality of ordinary life. Yet within this experienced reality it constitutes a signal of transcendence, because its intrinsic intention points beyond itself."[23]

# DISSIDENT PROTESTANT THEOLOGIANS

Thomas Aquinas's way of thinking about play and its relationship to the spiritual life is in marked contrast to that of the Puritans. If Thomas had been living in the United States during any part of our history, his views would have been well outside the mainstream, which probably explains why Catholics in America who had been influenced by him were perceived as so different by the Protestant majority. But some American Protestant theologians and ministers have held views that dissent from the Puritan heritage and the mainstream attitudes toward work and play in the United States as well. Unitarian minister Edward Everett Hale, for example, in the 1855 sermon *Public Amusement for Poor and Rich* questioned the religious views that sanctioned and legitimated the harsh conditions then typical of factories, only to serve the "idol of production." He was concerned that religion had become so closely identified with an emphasis on sobriety and industriousness that play had to go underground in American culture. The typical attitude, in his view, was that a person of "business character" was not expected to do anything so frivolous as to play. "I am afraid it would be thought a severe strain on business character," he wrote, "if it was whispered that a bank director or a member of the board of alderman, or a young lawyer, or a judge, were seen playing in a game of cricket, or joining in a rowing match of an afternoon. If they indulge in such levities at all, it must be before sunrise or after sunset."[24] Congregationalist minister Washington Gladden argued as well for a balanced approach to life that recognized the importance of both work and play. In his late nineteenth-century sermon "Amusements: Their Uses and Abuses" he comments that "no man is able to keep his faculties constantly in working tension. They must be relaxed occasionally, not only in rest, but also in play. Amusement is therefore as much a part of the divine economy as prayer, and one can glorify God by play, as well as by work or by worship."[25]

Congregationalist minister Horace Bushnell, the pioneer of liberal theology in New England, is another exemplar of this perspective. In his 1855 book *Christian Nurture*, about raising children in the Christian life, he critiqued the Puritan approach with its emphasis on industriousness and its neglect of play and enjoyment. For Bushnell, a child who had never experienced play would have a difficult time understanding the liberty that God's grace brings about in the Christian life. Indeed, for Bushnell, "play is the symbol and interpreter of liberty, that is, Christian liberty."[26]

For Bushnell, it is because of God's goodness that he has set our life up in such a way that our enjoyment in play as children helps to lead us to a life of grace:

> Therefore God has purposely set the beginning of the natural life in a mood that foreshadows the last and highest chapter of immortal character....He prepares at the very beginning of our life, in the free self-impulsion of play, that which is to foreshadow the glorious liberty of the soul's ripe order and attainment in good.[27]

Closer to our own time, Baptist theologian Harvey Cox has lamented the disappearance in Western industrialized nations of the medieval feast of fools and festivity in general, which he understands as a form of play. In his book *The Feast of Fools*, Cox echoes Thomas's point about the similarity between play and contemplation when he writes, "In my view, not only are prayer and play analogous but their kinship provides us with a sound contemporary access both to our religious tradition and to the future."[28]

In our present world it is also crucial for rich Western nations to recover something of their capacity for sympathetic imagination and non-instrumental joie de vivre if they are to keep in touch with the so-called "underdeveloped world." Otherwise, the rich Western nations will become increasingly static and provincial or they will try to inflict their worship of work on the rest of the world.[29]

It should be clear from this cursory overview of the thought of dissenting Protestant theologians that play and sport are topics about which there is considerable room for ecumenical collaboration. It will be important for Catholic theologians to bring the resources of their own heritage on this topic into dialogue with perspectives from our country's Protestant theologians, both past and present. Perhaps in working together to safeguard the dignity of the human person and the well-being and spiritual growth of our young people, we can find common ground that would otherwise elude us.

# THE IMPORTANCE OF INTERDISCIPLINARY STUDIES

Future research and reflection on play should also be interdisciplinary. Theologians should be in dialogue with scholars in disciplines such as philosophy, anthropology, and psychology, in which a great deal of research and writing has been done about play and sport. There is the classic work of Johan Huizinga, *Homo Ludens: A Study of the Play Element in Culture.*[30] But others have done very important scholarship about play and sport closer to our own time. I am thinking, for example, of the book *Sport, Play and Ethical Reflection* by philosopher Randolph Feezell.[31] In this book, Feezell makes a very persuasive case that sport is, at its heart, "enjoyment in play" and that most people engage in it for intrinsic reasons. He has a very sophisticated account, influenced by the writings of philosopher Frithjof Bergmann, of what it means to say that play is a free activity. In Feezell's understanding, even work can be like play, to the extent that the person is identifying with the activity and the activity gives expression to his or her "true self." Feezell's discussion of work as play and as an expression of one's "true self" opens up interesting possibilities for a new understanding of the meaning of "vocation."[32]

Psychologist Mihaly Csikszentmihalyi has also done important research on play in our own time. Indeed, conversations he had with people who were engaged in games and sports were foundational for the development of his groundbreaking "flow" theory. According to Csikszentmihalyi, the flow experience is associated with human well-being and flourishing and occurs most often when people are engaged in enjoyable activities that they do for their own sake. When people are engaged in such activities, they say that they experience a one-pointedness of mind, an egolessness, an increased sense of union with their surroundings, effortlessness (which is preceded by discipline), and an alteration of sense of time. The dynamics of the flow experience are very similar to the dynamics of the spiritual life as described by theologians and spiritual writers in the religious traditions of the world. Csikszentmihalyi's flow theory is important for theologians because it provides a way of understanding how the experience of play in sport can lead to the integral development of the person, including his or her spiritual growth.[33]

# THE CORRUPTION OF SPORT AND INTRINSIC REWARDS

As we have seen, according to Thomas Aquinas and Romano Guardini, play is similar to contemplation because both activities are enjoyable and done for their own sake. Feezell and Csikszentmihalyi both highlight the importance of these aspects of play, from the vantage points of philosophy and psychology respectively. As has been mentioned, in our society, sport has become connected in significant ways to extrinsic goods. Youth sport has become instrumentalized and considered in light of possible college scholarships or (for the more ambitious) professional contracts. Elite-level and professional sport is connected in more direct and obvious ways to extrinsic goods such as wealth and status.

But this is not to say that elite or professional sports are inherently corrupt. Or that it is not possible for a person to be fully committed to participation at a high level in sport and also be a Christian or a profoundly religious person. Recall Augustine's insight that corruption (or evil, in his terms) has to do with harming something that is good. As he put it, "A defect is against nature, because it harms a nature, and it would not harm it if it did not lessen its goodness. Therefore, evil is only a privation of good. Thus it never exists except in some good thing...."[34]

For Phil Jackson and Ignatius, corruption happens in sport as persons become "ensnared" (Ignatius's word) or attached to wealth and fame, which leads to "blinding pride" and then to all other vices. However, wealth and fame are extrinsic goods when it comes to sport; they are not a part of sport practices themselves. According to Phil Jackson, most successful athletes begin participating in their sport when they are young, because of their love of the game. In his view, this love of the game continues to be important to NBA players:

Whether they're willing to acknowledge it or not, what drives most basketball players is not the money or the adulation, but their love of the game. They live for moments when they can lose themselves completely in the action and experience the pure joy of competition.[35]

In Jackson's view, "one of the main jobs of a coach is to reawaken that spirit."[36] This love and passion for the sport itself is a fundamental part of the success of any great athlete or coach, even at the highest levels. The best coaches, like the best teachers, have a passion for what they are teaching, and for all of its nuances and fine points. They have a burning commitment to excellence in their spheres of expertise. And that comes across to their players or students.

It is common for successful athletes to experience a tension between attachment to wealth and fame and pure involvement in their sport for its own rewards. Seven-time world billiards champion Geet Sethi describes this tension very well in his book *Success vs Joy*. When he was growing up, he says, billiards was a form of meditation for him. When he was playing the game, he was lost to everything else and experienced joy. But that all changed once he became successful.

Winning the professional world championship (my third world title) made me a public figure and all that goes with it. There were material rewards as well. I started wearing a Rolex and got myself a big new car. I started becoming influenced by other people, especially those who are rich and powerful. With recognition and riches at the age of 32, came a corruption in lifestyle. It came insidiously but enveloped me.[37]

He writes about how at this time he no longer was exhilarated by joyous feelings. His concentration had been disturbed. "The game was no longer the end but a means toward achieving the end," he points out.[38] He went through a phase of soul searching and says that the answers began to appear before him. As he puts it, "I turned to the joys of living for the moment. To me this is the only way to be."[39]

Sethi now shares the insights he has gained from his own experiences in sport with others. In a chapter of his book entitled "The Corruption of Joy," he writes that "if joy disappears, all the efforts that you have made to become a master of your area of endeavor are rendered meaningless." And, for him, "joy disappears when your mind is distracted."

> You might be playing well, but if your mind is wavering —that is, you are thinking about publicity, the adulation of your fans or even about earning big bucks—your game is bound to suffer.[40]

Even in elite-level and professional sports, then, the humanly significant aspects of participation in sports have to do with enjoyment and participating in the activity for its own sake. The athlete who still enjoys his or her sport for its intrinsic rewards will continue to be motivated to practice and in the long run will play better. In other words, there is continuity in an experiential sense from the humanly significant aspects of participation in sport, even at elite and professional levels, to the dynamics of the spiritual life as these have been described by theologians such as Thomas Aquinas, Romano Guardini, and Harvey Cox.

# CONCLUSION

Ample support exists, both from cultural practices and theological principles, for Catholic theologians to begin reflecting on sport as an aspect of culture in the contemporary context. After all, contrary to the impression one gets from reading much of the history of sport in the West, Catholics are not late-comers to this aspect of culture. Indeed, they have been engaged in play and sport for well over a millennium. In medieval and early modern periods, play and sport were engaged in on feast days and Sundays, depicted in art on stained glass windows and in prayer books, incorporated into educational institutions and reflected on by some of the most prominent theologians. Catholics brought these cultural traditions with them to the United States, where they engaged in play and sport routinely and without anxiety and incorporated them in their schools as a matter of course.

The Catholic tendency to accept sport is based, in part, on the emphasis of theologians on the goodness of the material world and that the human person is a unity of body and soul or body, soul, and spirit. Another reason for the Catholic tendency to accept sport has to do with the way theologians understood the relationship between faith and culture. St. Paul was a foundational figure in this regard. As the apostle to the Gentiles, he spent most of his life making the gospel message known to the Greek-speaking world. And his approach involved referencing aspects of the Greek cultural heritage, including their sports. John Paul II draws on St. Paul's approach in encouraging Catholics in our own time to accept sport and to regard it with respect and esteem. For him, it is important to work to correct and elevate sport so that it serves the human person and his or her integral development, including in the area of spirituality.

And so one can retrieve theological principles from earlier periods that offer reasons for Catholic theologians to pay attention to sport in our contemporary context. One of the more interesting aspects of this topic, however, is that it is not only about abstract theological ideas that are unrelated to cultural realities and lived human experience. On the contrary, what was happening "on the ground," in the bodily practices of lay Catholics, was the most important part of the story told in this book. Lay Catholics were the bearers of the traditions that were subsequently rejected by the reformers and, in an emphatic way, by the Puritans. These rejections are still influencing us today and are related to some of the seemingly intractable problems in contemporary sport. We search for resources or ways of thinking that will help us out of these problems, often to no avail, it seems. But we have not yet looked into what we tossed aside, beginning with the Puritans and then in our subsequent history. We may have thought that we could simply return to the original meaning of scripture, or start with a clean slate with respect to knowledge (Descartes), and that this would lead us to salvation or to understanding of the truth without prejudice. But, in fact, we are still influenced by the past, which is (whether we like it or not) *our* past. And we are influenced by it precisely *in our rejection of it.*

The Puritans at Harvard in the early years were taken with the thought of Peter Ramus, who was a serious critic of Aristotle. And while Aristotle was a part of the classical curriculum in American liberal arts colleges, this began to change after the Civil War and at the time of increasing industrialization, to such an extent that it was no longer possible to assume a college graduate was familiar with Aristotle's ethics as we entered the twentieth century. Of course, there was good reason to reject aspects of Aristotle's thought because of what scientists were learning about the natural world. But perhaps Aristotle was on to something in his understanding of moderation as central to a virtuous life. For Thomas Aquinas, the humanists, and early Jesuits, this meant that a person should not be studying, working, or even praying all the time. A virtuous life also requires time for play and enjoyment, which provide "recreation and rest" for the soul. A retrieval of the emphasis on moderation in this sense is very helpful in resolving some of the problems that plague youth sport today, including both its overseriousness and the dramatic rise in overuse injuries.

The emphasis on moderation of one's desires is also helpful for addressing problems that plague intercollegiate, elite, and professional sport. If athletes at these levels can learn how to "recreate and relax" in a way that is sustaining and even spiritually nourishing, perhaps this can reduce the number of problems they have off the playing fields and courts. And, if moderation can be introduced into the desire to win, perhaps we will see fewer scandals involving performance-enhancing drug use and the violation of NCAA rules by intercollegiate athletic programs.

When considering our own context in the United States, it is important to recognize that cultures are not monolithic. And even the United States of the nineteenth century, which was predominantly Protestant, was not of a single mind about play and sport. Some of the more prominent Protestant ministers of the period rejected the Puritan heritage and argued vigorously for moderation in work. They emphasized that play, too, was a part of the Christian life and was even related to spiritual values. In other words, they sounded much more like Thomas Aquinas than Richard Baxter. A contemporary theologian such as Harvey Cox continues this tradition when he argues that play and prayer are analogous activities that provide us with access to our religious heritage and point the way forward to the future.

After the publication of Johan Huizinga's *Homo Ludens: A Study of the Play Element in Culture*, scholars in other disciplines, such as anthropology, philosophy, and psychology, have also written extensively about play. This scholarship should be taken seriously by any Catholic theologian who is interested in reflecting on the play element in sport in our own context. Of course, as Klaus Meier puts it, "for those who inhabit a world of total work, a call to play will sound socially immoral, 'as though directed at the very foundations of human society.'"[41] In this sense, a call to play is countercultural, at least with respect to the mainstream culture in the United States. The call to play sounds immoral because play is regarded as useless in a society that tells us to make ourselves useful—by being a productive participant in the consumer society. Contemplation and liturgy are "useless" in this sense as well. But this doesn't mean that they aren't important. The experiences of play and contemplation, after all, help to remind us that there is more to us—and to life—than our contribution to the gross national product or what we buy and sell. Indeed, perhaps it is through experiences of play that many of us are first drawn to contemplation, and to the praise of the God "who gives joy to our youth."[42]

# NOTES

## INTRODUCTION

1. "The Church," *Papal Teachings* (Boston: Daughters of St. Paul, 1960), p. 22.

## CHAPTER 1: "NO PURITAN PALL HOVERED OVER SUNDAYS"

The chapter title is a quotation from *Sports in the Western World* by William Baker.

1. Richard McBrien, *Catholicism* (San Francisco: HarperSanFrancisco, 1994), 1196.

2. George Sage, ed., *Sport and American Society: Selected Readings* (Reading, MA: Addison-Wesley, 1974), p. 5.

3. I discuss the work of scholars who understand the history of sport in the West in more detail in chapter 3. For now see, for example, D. Stanley Eitzen and George H. Sage, "Religion and Sport," in *Religion and Sport: The Meeting of Sacred and Profane*, Charles S. Prebish, ed. (Westport, CT: Greenwood, 1993), pp. 80–117, and Clifford Wallace Putney, *Muscular Christianity: The Strenuous Mood in American Protestantism, 1880–1920* (Cambridge, MA: Harvard University Press, 2001), esp. pages 50–51.

4. Irenaeus, "Against Heresies," in *Irenaeus of Lyons*, Robert M. Grant, ed., The Early Church Fathers (New York: Routledge, 1997), p. 172.

5. Ibid., pp. 164–65.

6. David N. Power, *Irenaeus of Lyons on Baptism and Eucharist: Selected Texts*, Alcuin/GROW Liturgical Study 18, Grove Liturgical Study #65 (Bramcote, UK: Grove Books, 1991), p. 21.

7. Thomas Aquinas, *Summa Contra Gentiles, Book 4: Salvation*, Charles J. O'Neil, trans. (Notre Dame, IN: University of Notre Dame Press, 1975), p. 247.

8. John of Damascus, *On the Divine Images: Three Apologies Against Those Who Attack the Divine Images*, David Anderson, trans. (Crestwood, NY: St. Vladimir's Seminary Press, 2000), p. 36.

9. William J. Baker, *Sports in the Western World* (Totowa, NJ: Rowman and Littlefield, 1982), p. 45. In the last two paragraphs I focus on lay Catholics, in part because they are often not included in scholarship about the history of spirituality. But it is well known that clerics participated in many popular religious practices alongside lay people in medieval Europe.

10. John Northbrooke, *A TREATISE wherein Dicing, Daunceing, Vaine playes, or Enterluds, with other idle pastimes, &c. commonly used on the Sabboth day, are reproved by the Authoritie of the word of God and auntient writers (London)*, 1577, p. 44. William Baker points out that the Puritan rejection of the recreational life of the people of England was intimately linked to their rejection of the Catholic feast days and holy days:

> The Puritans opposed the recreational life of the masses of Englishmen because it was geared to a seasonal cycle associated with the old Catholic church calendar. Various saints' days, the twelve days of Christmas, Plough Monday (the first Monday after the Twelfth Day), Shrove Tuesday, Easter, May Day, and Whitsuntide (forty days after Easter)—all were occasions for common folk to play football, stoolball, quoits, and bowls; to engage in dancing, boxing and wrestling matches, and running, jumping and throwing contests; and to gamble on bull baits, bear baits, and cockfights. (Baker, *Sports in the Western World*, pp. 76–77).

11. William Bradford, *On Plymouth Plantation: 1620–1647* (New York: Random House, 1981), p. 107.

12. Baker, *Sports in the Western World*, p. 83. In much scholarship about the history of Christianity the assumption has been that because the modern world (especially in England and America) was so shaped by the Reformation, the initiatives associated with it must have been popular in their own time. And yet, on examination of the historical evidence in England, such an assumption does not appear to be well founded. As Eamon Duffy has shown in his book, *The Stripping of the Altars: Traditional Religion in England 1400–1580* (New Haven and London: Yale University Press, 1992), there was not as deep a divide between the clerics and the people in late medieval England as subsequent writers of this history often suggest. Rather, the people's "spiritual" life was generally the traditional one described earlier in this chapter, and the priest played a central role, given his connection to the liturgy and the sacraments (see *The Stripping of the Altars*, esp. intro., and chap. 3). Another factor that the common analysis overlooks is how attached people can become to their bodily and ritual practices. To have these changed by government mandate was, in fact, disturbing to many Christians. There were many people in England, like those whom Governor Bradford encountered in the early colonies, who wanted to continue to "play, openly" as they had for centuries.

13. Samuel Eliot Morrison writes in his book *Harvard in the Seventeenth Century*, "In the matter of lawful recreations for Harvard students before 1674, the historian must confess to drawing the records almost blank. The puritans, with their emphasis on the virtue of hard work and the sin of idleness, overlooked the physical need of a young scholar for rest and recreation. Their only grievance against their mother universities (aside from the 'prelatical' atmosphere) was the 'waste of precious time' by students who were not kept almost constantly at their books and stated exercises" (Cambridge, MA: Harvard University Press, 1936, p. 112). The "mother universities" Morrison refers to are English universities, such as Oxford and Cambridge.

14. Etolia S. Basso, ed., *The World from Jackson Square: A New Orleans Reader* (New York: Farrar, Straus, 1948), p. 139.

15. Edward Everett Hale, *Public Amusement for Poor and Rich* (Boston: Phillips, Sampson and Co., 1857), p. 5.

16. Bernard Lonergan, "Theology in Its New Context," in *Renewal of Religious Thought*, L. K. Shook, ed. (Montreal: Palm Publishers, 1968), p. 34.

17. Charles Taylor, *A Secular Age* (Cambridge, MA: Belknap Press of Harvard University, 2007), p. 771.

18. "The Church," *Papal Teachings* (Boston: Daughters of St. Paul, 1960), p. 22.

19. Ibid.

20. I am not trying to absolve the church from responsibility for these developments. I am merely trying to understand how the leadership of the Catholic Church came to view so many of the developments of the modern world with such grave suspicion. As Andrew Greeley has observed, after all, it is clericalism that tends to bring about anticlericalism. The reactionary and defensive approach of the church toward the modern world, which insisted emphatically on the authority of church over state, religion over science, clerics over laity, soul over body, and so on, only deepened the rift between the church and culture in the modern period, which had significant negative repercussions in the pastoral area.

21. See "Pope Pius IX: Syllabus of Errors, 8 December 1864," in *Readings in Church History*, 3 vols in 1, Colman J. Barry, OSB, ed. (Westminster, MD: Christian Classics, 1985), pp. 992–95; and "Encyclical, 'Pascendi Dominici Gregis,' Condemning the Doctrines of Modernism, 8 September 1907," in *Readings in Church History*, pp. 1030–37. For the condemnations of Americanism, see specifically the "Apostolical Letter *Testem Benevolentia*, Jan. 22, 1899, addressed to His Eminence Cardinal Gibbons, Archbishop of Baltimore," in *The Great Encyclical Letters of Pope Leo XIII* (New York: Benziger Brothers, 1903), pp. 441–53.

22. See, for example, Gerald R. Gems, "The Prep Bowl: Football and Religious Acculturation in Chicago, 1927–1963," *Journal of Sport History* 23, no. 3 (Fall 1996): 284–302; Mark S.

Massa, *Catholics and American Culture: Fulton Sheen, Dorothy Day, and the Notre Dame Football Team* (New York: Crossroad, 1999), especially chap. 9, "Thomism and the T-Formation in 1966: Ethnicity, American Catholic Higher Education, and the Notre Dame Football Team"; and Julie Byrne, *O God of Players: The Story of the Immaculata Mighty Macs*, Religion and American Culture (New York: Columbia University Press, 2003).

# CHAPTER 2: "THE EARTH IS SHAKING WITH FLYING FEET"

The chapter title is a quotation from William Fitzstephen, *Medieval, Humanist, and Early Jesuit Practices.*

1. William Fitzstephen, "Description of the City of London," in *English Historical Documents, 1042–1189*, D. C. Douglas and G. W. Greenaway, eds., Vol. 2 (New York: Oxford University Press, 1953), pp. 956–62.

2. John Stow, *A Survey of London: Written in the Year 1598* (Gloucestershire, UK: Sutton Publishing, 2005). A few of the sports Fitzstephen mentions were no longer practiced during Stow's time or underwent changes during the four intervening centuries. And other new sports and customs were introduced. The one thing that remains constant, however, is the close connection between religious rituals and celebrations and the playing of games and sports.

3. Fitzstephen, "Description," p. 956. According to John Marshall Carter, Thomas Becket was an avid sportsman himself: "Among other things, the Archbishop of Canterbury was a true sportsman. Three of his biographers have pointed this out quite clearly. Yes, before and after his ecclesiastical position, Becket never lost interest in sports....He was extremely knowledgeable of hunting and falconry" (John Marshall Carter, *Sports and Pastimes of the Middle Ages* [Lanham, MD: University Press of America, 1988], p. 41).

4. Fitzstephen, "Description," pp. 959–60.

5. Ibid., pp. 960–62.

6. Ibid., p. 960. Some recent research is calling into question earlier assumptions about sports and recreations in late medieval and early modern English schools. Steve Bailey, in an article about Winchester College in England from 1382 to 1680 ("Permission to Play: Education for Recreation and Distinction at Winchester College, 1382–1680," *International Journal of the History of Sport* 12, no. 1 [April 1995]: 1–17) writes that there has been much scholarship on aspects of physical activity in the English public schools in the nineteenth century, but when writers consider earlier periods, the assumption tends to be that "physical activity in schools was haphazard and even barbaric. It is reported to have been tolerated by authorities, but certainly not encouraged by them" (Bailey, "Permission to Play," p. 1). Contrary to this picture, he found that at Winchester College, founded in 1382 by William of Wykeham, bishop of Winchester, "opportunities for recreation were consistently maintained from the founding of the College, and these were later expanded" (p. 2). In addition to the opportunities for games and sports, he remarks on the surprising "extent to which the Wardens and Fellows were keen to expose their pupils to the entertainments and diversions of the ruling classes. Visits by jugglers, jesters, minstrels, various musicians and actors" were an integral part of the life of the school and were sponsored and encouraged by the authorities (p. 2). "The dark and bleak picture," he writes, "of repressive clerics strictly enforcing an ascetic regime on the Winchester scholars cannot be maintained" (p. 7).

7. Fitzstephen, "Description," pp. 960–61.

8. Ibid., p. 961.

9. Ibid.

10. John Stow, *A Survey of London*, pp. 96–97.

11. Ibid., p. 97.

12. Ibid., p. 99.

13. Ibid.

14. Ibid., p. 100.

15. Ibid., p. 101.

16. Ibid., p. 98.

17. Philip Stubbes, *The Anatomie of Abuses* (London, 1583), sigs L2–L4v.

18. Natalie Zemon Davis, *Society and Culture in Early Modern France* (Stanford, CA: Stanford University Press, 1975), p. 98.

19. Ibid.

20. Allen Guttmann, *Women's Sports: A History* (New York: Columbia University Press, 1991), pp. 47–48.

21. Baker, *Sports in the Western World*, p. 48. According to Guttmann, medieval football as it was played by women was every bit as rough as it was among men: "They pushed, shoved kicked, and frolicked with as much reckless abandon as their fathers, brothers, husbands and sons; and they seem to have suffered as many broken bones and cracked crowns as the men did" (Guttmann, *Women's Sports*, p. 48). For Teresa McLean, "a sport had to be very rough indeed before it was too rough for medieval women, who played and disported, as they hunted and worked, alongside the men" (Teresa McLean, *The English at Play in the Middle Ages* [Shooter's Lodge, Windsor Forest, UK: Kensal Press, 1983], p. 7).

22. See Guttmann, *Women's Sports*, pp. 48–52.

23. Ibid., p. 47.

24. I am following Paul Oskar Kristeller's definition of a humanist. See Paul Oskar Kristeller, "The Humanist Movement," in *Renaissance Thought and Its Sources* (New York: Columbia University Press, 1979).

25. There were also Protestant humanists, of course, after 1517. The humanists I consider in this chapter, in Italy and France, were Catholic, and their religious faith influenced how they understood and went about the task of educating youth.

26. Jacob Burckhardt, *The Civilization of the Renaissance in Italy* (London: Phaidon, 1950). See Paul Oskar Kristeller, "Paganism and Christianity," in *Renaissance Thought and Its Sources*.

27. See Guttmann, *Women's Sports*, pp. 62–66, for a lengthier discussion about women's sports during this period. In these pages, Guttmann quotes Werner Korbs, who writes about the Venetian regatta:

Understandably, the women's regatta enjoyed special popularity. The participants were peasant women of the area—especially from Pellestrina—who had plenty of practice thanks to weekly boat trips to the market in Venice....Antonio Gabellico reported of the first official women's regatta in 1493, to celebrate the arrival of Beatrice d'Este, that the fifty competing peasant maids in their short linen skirts made a strong impression and that the spectacle, as unfamiliar as it was charming, greatly diminished the effects of the men's spectacle which followed. (Werner Korbs, *Vom Sinn der Leibesubungen zur Zeit der italienischen Renaissance*, Wolfgang Decker, ed. [Hildesheim: Weidmann, 1988], pp. 26–27; quoted in Guttmann, *Women's Sports*, in English translation, pp. 65–66).

28. Guttmann, *Women's Sports*, p. 70.

29. Ibid.

30. See John W. O'Malley, *Trent and All That: Renaming Catholicism in the Early Modern Era* (Cambridge, MA: Harvard University Press, 2000), p. 136. O'Malley also notes that the Ursulines were only one of several religious communities of women who operated schools for girls in France in the seventeenth century.

31. *Isocrates I*, Michael Gagarin, ed., David Mirhady and Yun Lee Too, trans., *The Oratory of Classical Greece*, Vol. 4 (Austin: University of Texas Press, 2004), p. 238.

32. For this reason, Daniel Dombrowski points out that it is "anachronistic to view Plato as a Cartesian" in his approach to education. In this area, he shows himself to be as much of a hylomorphist—someone who views the human person as a unity of body and soul—as Aristotle (Daniel A. Dombrowski, *Contemporary Athletics and Ancient Greek Ideals* [Chicago: University of Chicago Press, 2009], p. 25).

33. Quoted in Johan Huizinga, *Homo Ludens: a Study of the Play Element in Culture* (Boston: Beacon Press, 1968), pp. 18–19.

34. William Harrison Woodward, *Vittorino da Feltre and Other Humanist Educators* (London: C. J. Clay and Sons, 1897), p. 32.

35. Ibid., 65. According to Woodward, Vittorino did not want his pupils to be "eggheads" prematurely. "Two little boys were overheard by him talking earnestly apart; hearing that they were discussing their lessons, he exclaimed, 'That is not a good sign in a young boy,' and sent them off to join the games" (Woodward, *Vittorino Da Feltre*, p. 35).

36. Burckhardt, *The Civilization of the Renaissance in Italy*, p. 235.

37. Aristotle, *Nichomachean Ethics*, J.A.K. Thomas, trans. (New York: Penguin Classics, 1984), p. 100.

38. Aeneas Silvius Piccolomini, "The Education of Boys," in *Humanist Educational Treatises*, Craig W. Kallendorf, ed. and trans., The I Tatti Renaissance Library (Cambridge, MA: Harvard University Press, 2002), p. 143. In another context, Piccolomini writes that the young should "not be restrained too closely or they will become listless and lazy. They should be allowed to play and their pleasure should be indulged somewhat; this activity will summon forth their qualities of spirit and heart, they will come to distinguish good from bad, and will learn to detect the snares of the world and how to avoid them when they have gained maturity" (*Selected Letters of Aeneas Silvius Piccolomini*, Albert R. Baca, ed. and trans. [Northridge, CA: San Fernando Valley State College, 1969], p. 20). Piccolomini (1405–64) was elected pope in 1458 and served as Pope Pius II until his death in 1464. Other theologians and leaders of the church during this time wrote about the importance of physical education and sports for young people. The Augustinian monk Maffeo Vegio (1407–58) addressed this topic in one of the more influential books of the time, *De educatione liberorum et eorum claris moribus*. Cardinal Jacopo Sadeloto (1477–1547) did so in the educational treatise *De Liberis Recte Instituendis* in 1530, as did Cardinal Silvio Antoniano (1540–1603) in his *Tre libri dell' educasione cristiana de' figliuoli* in 1584.

39. Pier Paolo Vergerio, "The Character and Studies Befitting a Free-Born Youth," in *Humanist Educational Treatises*, p. 83.

40. Ibid., p. 85.

41. Ibid., p. 77.

42. Jacob Burckhardt highlights the important role of the humanists in Italy with respect to our topic. "In the sixteenth century the Italians had all Europe for their pupils both theoretically and practically in every noble bodily exercise and in the habits and manners of good society. Their instructions and their illustrated books on riding, fencing, and dancing served as the model to other countries" (*The Civilization of the Renaissance in Italy*, p. 235).

43. Michel de Montaigne, *The Essays: A Selection*, Michael Screech, ed. and trans. (New York: Penguin Books, 1987, 1991), p. 60.

44. Ibid., p. 59.

45. Ibid. For Montaigne, even the studies themselves would bear more fruit if they were approached in a playful manner. He discusses how his own father taught him: "As for Greek,...my father planned to have it taught to me methodically, but in a new way, as a sort of game or sport. We would bounce declensions about, rather like those who use certain board-games as a means of learning arithmetic or geometry. For among other things he had been counseled to bring me to love knowledge and duty by my own choice, without forcing my will, and to educate my soul entirely through gentleness and freedom" (Montaigne, *The Essays*, pp. 69–70).

46. Ibid., pp. 72–73.

47. Phillipe Aries, *Centuries of Childhood: A Social History of Family Life* (New York: Vintage Books, 1962), p. 88.

48. Ibid.

49. Francois de Dainville, *L'Education des Jesuites: XVI–XVIII siecles* (Paris: Editions de Minuit, 1978), p. 518. The information having to do with Jesuit schools in France in the next several paragraphs is based on Dainville's book. See especially the chapters "L'exercise physique dans les colleges de l'ancien regime" (pp. 518–25) and "Les vacances dans l'ancienne france" (pp. 526–33).

50. Ibid., p. 520.

51. Ibid., pp. 520–21.

52. *The Jesuit Ratio Studiorum of 1599*, trans. with intro and notes by Allan P. Farrell, SJ (Washington, DC: Conference of Major Superiors of Jesuits, 1970), p. 12.

53. Ibid., p. 12.

54. Dainville, *L'Education des Jesuites*, p. 519.

55. Ibid.

56. Ibid.

57. Cited in *L'Education des Jesuites*, p. 519. The passage is from Cardinal Antoniano's *Tre libri dell' educasione cristiana de' figliuoli*, published in 1584.

58. This was the game mentioned earlier in the chapter that Borgia recommended in which players used a mallet to hit a wooden ball through an iron hoop. Americans, think croquet.

59. Dainville, *L'Education des Jesuites*, pp. 524–25.

60. Ibid, 524. This young Jesuit was not pleased with what he was observing. He seemed to think the students were spending too much time playing games and sports and not enough time on their studies.

61. Aries, *Centuries of Childhood*, p. 89.

62. Ibid.

63. Ibid. After the suppression of the Society of Jesus in 1773 and its restoration in 1814, the Jesuits in France continued to incorporate physical recreation and games into their schools. The author of an article published in the French paper *Le Figaro* in 1879 observed, "Games and amusements occupy an important place in the schools of the Jesuits. They are as much interested about the place of recreation as about the study hall. The prefects induce the pupils to join in the games with the same ardor they display in stimulating them to work at their books. Two prefects, Fathers de Nodaillac and Rousseau, have written the history of games..." (Aries, *Centuries of Childhood*, p. 89).

64. Robert Schwickerath, *Jesuit Education: Its History and Principles Viewed in the Light of Modern Education Problems* (St. Louis: B. Herder, 1903), p. 573.

65. *Ignatius of Loyola: Letters and Instructions*, Martin E. Palmer, SJ, John W. Padberg, SJ, John L. McCarthy, SJ, eds., no. 23 in Series I: Jesuit Primary Sources in English Translations (St. Louis: Institute of Jesuit Sources, 2006), pp. 254–55.

66. Ibid., p. 255.

67. Ibid.

68. *Monumenta Paedagogica Societatis Jesu/penitus retractata multisque textibus aucta*, Ladislaus Lukacs, ed., Vol. 92, nos. 107–8 (Rome: Institutum Historicum Societatis Jesu, 1965), pp. 68–69.

69. Ibid., p. 70.

70. *The Constitutions of the Society of Jesus and Their Complementary Norms: A Complete English Translation of the Official Latin Texts*, John Padberg, SJ, ed., no. 15 in Series I: Jesuit Primary Sources in English Translation (St. Louis: Institute of Jesuit Sources, 1996), pp. 140 and 127. Judging from one report of the time, Ignatius's attention to the care of the body had very practical results. Luis Goncalves da Camara wrote in his *Memoriale*, "Our Father always takes the greatest care of the sick so that they can get better, and also for the healthy that they maintain their health; for this reason, in spite of there being some seventy men and more in the college, there are very seldom any sick and then only with slight ailments" (*Remembering Inigo: Glimpses of the Life of Saint Ignatius of Loyola, The Memoriale of Luis Goncalves da Camara*, trans. with intro., notes, and indices by Alexander Eaglestone and Joseph A. Munitiz, SJ, no. 19 in Series I: Jesuit Primary Sources in English Translation [Saint Louis: Institute of Jesuit Sources, 2004], p. 21).

71. Da Camara writes, "The villa is a small country estate which our Father (Ignatius) arranged to have bought at a time when we were in great need simply because it seemed necessary to him for the sake of the brethren's health" (Goncalves da Camara, *Remembering Inigo*, p. 83).

It is clear from his emphasis on the importance of the villa that Ignatius felt that all the Jesuits, not just the young, should take a break at times from their labors and have time for recreation. According to da Camara, he also insisted that any Jesuit coming to Rome take exercise each morning when he first arrived in the city, because of the potentially harmful effects of the local climate. In his *Memoriale*, da Camara wrote:

> Our Father used to order all the members of the Society who arrived in Rome for the first time to take

some exercise in the fresh air of Rome every morning before sunrise, so that the local climate, which is harmful to foreigners, should not harm them. Accordingly I was told as soon as I arrived that I also should take the same exercise. I did so for two or three days, and as I thought that it was not an order imposed by obedience or a rule to be observed by all those arriving from abroad, but only a permission given to me, I neglected to do so one of the days of the first week. Our Father heard of this and sent for me; he asked me why I had not gone to take exercise, and when he had heard my excuse he imposed as a penance that next Sunday I should eat at the "little table" and that Antonio Rion (an Italian brother coadjutor, and specialist in dressing people down) should reprimand me. (*Remembering Inigo*, p. 65)

72. Ibid., p. 105.

73. Ibid. Da Camara writes about a popular pastime at the villa, involving some of the fathers "playing games with oranges, throwing them to one another continually, with the one who dropped the orange having to say a Hail Mary on his knees" (*Remembering Inigo*, p. 105).

74. Francois Pierron, *Le Bon Precepteur ou La belle maniere de bien elever la jeunesse pour Dieu, & pour le beau monde* (Lyon: Chez Horace Boissat & G. Remers, 1661), p. 218.

75. Ibid., p. 216.

76. Ibid., p. 223.

77. Ibid., p. 221.

78. In Thomas L. Altherr, ed., *Sports in North America: A Documentary History, Vol. 1 Part I–Sports in the Colonial Era 1618–1783* (Gulf Breeze, FL: Academic International, 1997), p. 455.

79. Ibid.

80. Ibid., p. 87. The English word *savage* is the translation of the French word *sauvage*, which is derived from the Latin *silva*, meaning "forest." Originally, it meant a person or group of people who lived in the forest or the country and did not use complex technologies. This was the sense in which the Jesuits used the term

during this period. They did not mean by *savage* "less than human." In fact, the Jesuits missionaries are clear in their writings that the Native people are every bit as human as the French, and they condemn French people who think otherwise. The term *savage* as used by the Jesuits was not free of negative connotations, however. It was generally not a compliment, certainly not in France when uttered by a townsperson to refer to someone who was a forest dweller. While the Jesuits adopted the Native way of life in order to spread the gospel, they would also have shared the view of French townspeople that civility associated with settled life in a village, town or city was better than the "savage" way of life.

81. Ibid., pp. 437–38.

82. Joseph Francois Lafitau, *Customs of the American Indians Compared with the Customs of Primitive Times*, 2 vols., William N. Fenton, ed., and Elizabeth L. Moore, trans. (Toronto: Champlain Society, 1974). This book was first published in 1724.

83. In his Huxley Memorial Lecture of 1952, Kaj Birket-Smith remarked, "It is generally admitted that…Lafitau…took the first step toward ethnological research for its own sake" (cited in Lafitau, *Customs of the American Indians*, Vol. 1, p. xxix). And Alfred Metraux takes note of the fact that "the very outline of Lafitau's work corresponds to the table of contents of any modern anthropological textbook" (p. xxix). The level of detail with which Lafitau describes Native games can be seen in the following description of one of their ball games:

> After marking two goals far enough apart, as much as five hundred paces, the players assemble in the middle between these limits. The player who is to begin the game holds in his hand a ball larger but less compact than those used in our tennis games. He is supposed to throw it in the air as perpendicularly as he can in order to catch it when it falls again. All the others form a circle around him, holding their hands high above their heads to catch it also when it falls. The player who has been able to make himself master of it tries to reach one of the distant goals. The attention of the others is given to blocking him, barring his way, keeping him

from their goals, pushing him always back to the centre, finally to seizing him and taking the ball from him. But he, watching all their moves, dodges now to one side, now to the other, holding the ball always firmly grasped, seeking always to evade his pursuers, pushing and jostling all those who are in his way, until he sees himself in danger of being caught without possibility of escape. Then he is supposed to throw it to one of the fastest of the team who is in a position to defend it. But, to lengthen the match, he makes his skill consist in throwing it to those behind him farthest from the goal towards which he was moving, in deceiving them even, pretending to look one way and throwing it another. After this, from being pursued, he becomes in turn the pursuer and loses no hope of again catching the ball which passes in this way from hand to hand. This makes a very quick and agreeable diversion and one requiring skill. It continues until at last some more fortunate player reaches one of the goals. This constitutes the winning of the game which the players then begin over again in the same way. (Lafitau, *Customs of the American Indians*, Vol. 2, pp. 197–98)

84. Lafitau, *Customs of the American Indians,* Vol. 2, p. 189.
85. Ibid.
86. Ibid., p. 191.
87. Ibid., p. 195. Notice that Lafitau departs from the norm for Jesuits, in that he does not condemn gambling in this case.
88. Lafitau uses as his European sources for comparison the classics of Greek and Roman literature he would have studied as a youth in Jesuit schools and during his training in the Jesuits. He writes, for example:

The game of hand ball which is gymnastic is no less ancient than that of dice. Apollonius of Rhodes, after telling us how Cupid played the latter game with Ganymede, just as we described it, has him stop the game although he had all the advantage, on the hope which his mother Venus held out to him of making him the present of a fine ball—the same one which Jupiter had received from his nurse Adrasta, with whom this god had had his happiest childhood pleasures on the Island of Crete—provided that, on his side, he is willing to accord her the favour which she comes to ask him for Juno and Minerva.

Homer in the sixth and eighth book of the Odessey has the Phoeacians play it. In the first place it is Nausicaa, the king's daughter, who indulges in this diversion at the seashore with her followers. In the second, it is two young men who excelled in this art and to whom no one dared compare himself. By the order of Alcinuous, they dance alone while playing, and they do it with so much exactness and charm that they draw the applause of all those present at this spectacle. The ancients studied to give good grace to all their movements, which made ball games to be regarded as like an orchestral contest in which they gave lessons in the public gymnasium. (Lafitau, *Customs of the American Indians*, pp. 196–97)

89. Ibid., pp. 198–99.
90. Ibid., p. 199.

# CHAPTER 3: "THE SPIRIT IS BOUND WITH THE FLESH"

The chapter title is a quotation from "Against Heresies," in *Irenaeus of Lyons*, edited by Robert M. Grant.

1. D. Stanley Eitzen and George H. Sage, "Religion and Sport," in *Religion and Sport: The Meeting of Sacred and Profane*, Charles S. Prebish, ed. (Westport, CT: Greenwood, 1993), pp. 84–85.

2. Clifford Wallace Putney, *Muscular Christianity: The Strenuous Mood in American Protestantism, 1880–1920* (Cambridge, MA: Harvard University Press, 2001), p. 51. The quote within the quote is from Deobold B. Van Dalen et al., *A World History of*

*Physical Education* (Englewood Cliffs, NJ: Prentice Hall, 1971), pp. 97–98. I do not take the time to respond to each of the points made by these authors now. I simply present their views. It should be noted, however, that the more significant development during the medieval period was the incorporation of Aristotle into the curricula in the universities. And Aristotle emphasized that the human person was a unity of body and soul. But even Plato, as was mentioned in chapter 2, tended in this direction in his writings on education, which led him to emphasize the importance of the body and physical exercise and sport in education.

3. Ibid.

4. Allen Guttmann, *Women's Sports: A History* (New York: Columbia University Press, 1991), pp. 41–42.

5. Allen Guttmann, *The Erotic in Sports* (New York: Columbia University Press, 1996), p. 35.

6. Allen Guttmann, *From Ritual to Record: The Nature of Modern Sports* (New York: Columbia University Press, 1978), pp. 24–25. One wonders how the Greeks could have placed so much emphasis on the body and sport if one of their most important thinkers was as anti-body as Plato is thought to have been.

7. It is true that some writers in the Christian tradition write in a harsh or negative way about the material world and the human body. There is a tendency for some monastic authors to paint a picture of the world that is none too flattering and to emphasize the importance of withdrawing from the world for growth in the spiritual life. And since spiritual writing was dominated for so long by either monks or others living celibate lives, the whole area of sexuality is usually treated as a place of temptation rather than as a context within which the Christian spiritual life unfolds.

I am afraid some authors exaggerate the importance of such tendencies in the Christian tradition, however. Jean DeLemeau, for example, in his book *Sin and Fear* (Jean DeLemeau, *Sin and Fear: The Emergence of a Western Guilt Culture 13th–18th Centuries*, Eric Nicholson, trans. [New York: St. Martin's Press, 1990]), writes about the fear and dread that perils of many kinds introduced into the psyches of people in Europe in the late Middle Ages and the early modern period. But, according to DeLemeau, Western civilization was affected by "two supplementary and equally oppressive causes for alarm: the 'horror' of sin and the 'obsession' of damnation":

> The church's insistence on both of the latter eventually led an entire society to condemn material life and daily concerns. Whence the inspiration of hymns such as this one, sung in the beginning of the eighteenth century by the congregations of Grignion de Montfort:
>
> *Leave your wood awhile, carpenter,*
> *Put aside your iron, locksmith.*
> *Set down your work, craftsman*
> *Let us seek Grace.*
>
> Then, more than ever before, did the West's religion of "anxiety" differ from the Eastern religions of "tranquility": Hinduism and Buddhism. (DeLemeau, *Sin and Fear*, p. 3)

Unfortunately, this passage is typical of many in DeLemeau's book. He makes sweeping statements such as that the horror of sin and obsession with damnation "led an entire society to condemn material life and daily concerns" and follows such statements with a quote that does not support the generalization. Leaving the wood aside for a while, after all, is not yet condemning material life or daily concerns. And certainly Hindu and Buddhist spiritual teachers would suggest withdrawal from the busy affairs of the world from time to time. DeLemeau's portrayal, which leaves the impression that *contemptus mundi* and of the flesh is all there is to Christianity, is too one-sided—more one-sided than the Christian tradition itself, which includes both the more negative appraisals of the material world and the body and many other positive ones.

8. David Tracy's observation that the Catholic imagination is analogical or sacramental is very helpful for understanding the kind of religious culture that emerged in the medieval period (*The Analogical Imagination: Christian Theology and the Culture of*

*Pluralism* [New York: Crossroad, 1986]). According to Tracy, an analogical imagination tends to emphasize God's presence in the created world, or God's immanence. The classic works of Catholic theologians, he says, tend to give expression to such an imagination. But Catholic theologians themselves are giving theoretical expression to a sensibility that has its roots in lived, bodily experiences and cultural practices. As Andrew Greeley puts it:

> Catholics live in an enchanted world, a world of statues and holy water, stained glass and votive candles, saints and religious medals, rosary beads and holy pictures. But these Catholic paraphernalia are mere hints of a deeper and more pervasive religious sensibility which inclines Catholics to see the Holy lurking in creation. As Catholics, we find our houses and our world haunted by a sense that the objects, events, and persons of daily life are revelations of grace. (Andrew Greeley, *The Catholic Imagination* [Berkeley: University of California Press, 2000], p. 1)

I hope this chapter can contribute to our understanding of the central place of the body in religious cultures that are characterized by such an analogical imagination.

9. I am grateful to Louis A. Ruprecht for pointing out the way that contemporary interpretations of Christianity offered by scholars of sport resemble earlier interpretations of Christianity put forward by groups such as the Gnostics and Manicheans that were rejected by Christian theologians and the formal teaching of the church at the time.

10. *Oxford Dictionary of the Christian Church [ODCC]*, F. L. Cross and E. A. Livingstone, eds. (Oxford, UK: Oxford University Press, 1997), s.v. "Gnosticism." I am following the *ODCC* interpretation of Gnosticism in this section.

11. Ibid.

12. Irenaeus, "Against Heresies," in *Irenaeus of Lyons*, Robert M. Grant, ed., The Early Church Fathers (New York: Routledge, 1997), p. 64.

13. Ibid.

14. Justin Martyr, "Fragments of the Lost Work of Justin on the Resurrection," in *Ante-Nicene Fathers, Vol. 1: Justin Martyr and Irenaeus*, Rev. Alexander Roberts, DD, and James Donaldson, LLD, eds., rev. with notes by A. Cleveland Coke, Rev. M. Dods, MA, trans. (Grand Rapids, MI: Eerdmans, 1967), p. 295.

15. *ODCC*, s.v. "Gnosticism."

16. Irenaeus, "Against Heresies," p. 86. Irenaeus writes that Marcion "said there would be salvation only for souls that had learned his doctrine, while the body, taken from the earth, cannot share in salvation" (p. 96).

17. Ibid., pp. 87–88.

18. Ibid., p. 172.

19. Ibid., pp. 139–40. The views of theologians such as Eutyches (c. 378–454), who taught that there was only one nature in Christ and denied that his humanity was consubstantial with ours, were condemned by the church. According to church leaders, central to the error of these theologians was that they did not acknowledge that the Word received human *flesh* from Mary. In a letter pertaining to this controversy that Pope Leo wrote to the bishop of Constantinople in 450, the pope points out that Eutyches should have paid closer attention to Isaiah's preaching, *"Behold a virgin will receive in the womb and will bear a son, and they will call his name Emmanuel, which is translated 'God is with us,"* and other such passages:

> Then he would not deceive people by saying that the Word was made flesh in the sense that he emerged from the virgin's womb having a human form but not having the reality of his mother's body....It was the holy Spirit that made the virgin pregnant, but the reality of the body derived from body. As Wisdom built a house for herself, the Word was made flesh and dwelt among us: that is, in that flesh which he derived from human kind and which he animated with the spirit of a rational life. ("The Letter of Pope Leo to Flavian, bishop of Constantinople, about Eutyches," in *Decrees of Ecumenical Councils: Vol. I: Nicea I to Lateran V*, Norman P. Tanner, SJ, ed.

[Washington, DC: Georgetown University Press and London: Sheed and Ward, 1990], *78)

20. Irenaeus, "Against Heresies," p. 169.

21. Ibid., p. 167.

22. Ibid., pp. 167–68. For Irenaeus, if someone were to say that "the flesh of the Lord was different in substance from ours" he would be mistaken and would jeopardize the very conditions that made redemption possible. "If the Lord took flesh of another substance, what became hostile by transgression is not reconciled to God. But now by our communion with him the Lord reconciled man with the Father, reconciling us by the body of his flesh (Col. 1:22) and redeeming us by his blood, as the Apostle says to the Ephesians: 'In whom we have redemption through his blood, the remission of sins (1:7)'" (p. 169).

23. Ibid., p. 168.

24. Ibid.

25. Justin Martyr, "Fragments of the Lost Work of Justin on the Resurrection," pp. 297–98.

26. According to Steven Runciman, the alarm that the Manichean movement caused in the medieval period "was proved by the horror with which the word 'Manichean' came to be regarded. In the future, the average orthodox Christian, when faced with any sign of dualism, would cry out 'Manichean,' and everyone would know that here was rank heresy" (Steven Runciman, The Medieval Manichee: A Study of the Christian Dualist Heresy [Cambridge, UK: Cambridge University Press, 1955], p. 17).

27. Westminster Dictionary of Christian Spirituality, Gordon S. Wakefield, ed. (Philadelphia: Westminster, 1983), s.v. "Manichaeism." I am following the interpretation of Manichaeism in this article.

28. St. Augustine, "The Heresies," in Arianism and Other Heresies, John E. Rotelle, ed., intro., trans. and notes, Roland J. Teske, SJ, Works of Saint Augustine: A Translation for the 21st Century, Part I, Vol. 18 (New York: New City Press, 1995), p. 45.

29. St. Augustine, "The Morals of the Catholic Church," in Basic Writings of St. Augustine, Vol. 1, ed. with intro and notes, Whitney J. Oates (New York: Random House, 1948), p. 327.

30. Saint Augustine, *City of God*, Henry Bettenson, trans. (New York: Penguin Books, 2003), p. 455. This emphasis on the goodness of God's creation as described in the first chapter of Genesis would have a profound impact on Christian spirituality. Francis of Assisi, for example, was held up as an example for other Christians precisely because of the depth of his appreciation of the goodness of God's creation. As his contemporary biographer Thomas of Celano put it,

> He exhorted with the sincerest purity cornfields and vineyards, stones and forests and all the beautiful things of the fields, fountains of water and the green things of the gardens, earth and fire, air and wind, to love God and serve him willingly....In every work of the artist he praised the Artist; whatever he found in the things made he referred to the Maker. He rejoiced in all the works of the hands of the Lord and saw behind things pleasant to behold their life-giving reason and cause. In beautiful things he saw Beauty itself; all things were to him good. "He who made us is the best," they cried out to him. (Marie Dennis et al., *St. Francis and the Foolishness of God* [New York: Orbis Books, 1993, 8th ed., 2000], quoted on p. 106)

31. St. Augustine, "On Continence," xxii.26. Quoted in Margaret R. Miles, *Fullness of Life: Historical Foundations for a New Asceticism* (Philadelphia: Westminster, 1981), p. 147. Augustine and other early Christian writers rejected the view that the soul was a part of God, insisting that both body and soul were created by God. Augustine also rejected the view that the soul was associated with everything pure and good and spiritual and that the body was the source of all temptation and sinfulness. He writes in the *City of God*, "For anyone who exalts the soul as the Supreme Good, and censures the nature of the flesh as something evil, is in fact carnal alike in his cult of the soul and in his revulsion from the flesh, since this attitude is prompted by human folly, not by divine truth" (p. 554).

32. St. Augustine, *Confessions* (Indianapolis: Hackett , 2006), p. 127.

33. Ibid.

34. Augustine, "In Joannis Evangelium tractatus," xxvii.5. Quoted in Margaret Miles, *Augustine on the Body* (Missoula, MT: Scholars Press, 1979), pp. 7–8. Formal church teaching insisted that the "Word became flesh" and drew out the full implications of this belief. In 1208, for example, Pope Innocent III wrote up a "Profession of Faith" for the Waldensians, a group that had inherited the cosmological dualism of Mani, according to which matter was considered evil. This led the Waldensians, like the Manicheans, to teach that the body of Jesus was merely an appearance, not real. Innocent wrote in the "Profession":

> He was born of the Virgin Mary by a true birth in the flesh. He ate and drank, slept and rested when He was tired from walking. He suffered a true passion in the flesh, died His own true bodily death, rose again by a true resurrection of His flesh and the true resumption of His body by His soul. He ate and drank in His risen flesh.... (*The Christian Faith in the Documents of the Catholic Church*, 5th ed., J. Neuner, SJ, and J. Dupuis, SJ, eds. [New York: Alba House, 1990], p. 187)

35. Saint Augustine, *City of God*, 549. The scriptural quotation is from Galatians 5:19–21.

36. Ibid.

37. Ibid, p. 550.

38. Augustine, "Heresies," in *Arianism*, p. 46. The Manichean teaching that marriage and regeneration were evil was based on this same kind of dualistic mentality, which according to Augustine, contradicted the writings of the Apostle Paul. As he put it:

> What error, then—or, better, what utter madness—has possessed the Manichees, for them to class our flesh as belonging to some kind of mythical nation of darkness? They would have it to have been inherently evil always, without any beginning, despite the fact that the teacher of the truth exhorts husbands to love their wives on the model of their love for their own flesh, and exhorts them also to do it on the model of Christ's love for the Church? (St. Augustine, *Marriage*

*and Virginity*, John E. Rotelle, ed., Ray Kearney, trans., *The Works of Saint Augustine*, Part I, Vol. 9 (Hyde Park, NY: New City Press, 1999, p. 206).

In its formal teachings the church rejected the Manichean views on marriage and regeneration. See, for example, the Council of Braga of 561, "Anathematisms against the Priscillianists." The Priscillianists were a Manichean sect in Spain. "If anyone condemns human marriage and despises the procreation of children, as Manes and Priscillian have said, *anathema sit*" (*The Christian Faith*, p. 128). The bishops at the Second Lateran Council in 1215 wrote, "Not only virgins and the continent, but also married persons, by pleasing God through right faith and good work, merit to attain to eternal happiness" (*The Christian Faith*, p. 16).

39. According to Norman Williams, in the course of Christian history, the doctrine of the fall has been most emphasized in those periods when the church felt the need to combat dualism and pessimism. As he puts it, "It is the idea of the Fall, with its necessary implication of the contingency and temporality, as opposed to the eternity and necessity, of evil, which makes all the difference: without the belief in the Fall, the doctrine of Original Sin *is* Manichaeism....The Fall theory and dualism are in principle, and always have been in history, mutually exclusive hypotheses" (Norman P. Williams, *The Idea of the Fall and of Original Sin* [London: Longmans, 1927], p. 148).

40. St. Augustine, "Answer to an Enemy of the Law and the Prophets," in *Arianism and Other Heresies*, 360–61. He writes in another place, "Therefore good may exist on its own, but evil cannot. The natures which have been perverted as a result of the initiative of an evil choice, are evil in so far as they are vitiated, but in so far as they are natures, they are good" (*City of God*, p. 474).

41. St. Augustine, *City of God*, p. 569. In this book I am dealing with the Christian responses to Gnosticism and Manicheaism because at the heart of these controversies were questions pertaining to the material world and the human body. In his later writings against the Pelagians, Augustine emphasized the effects of original sin and the need for God's grace for all that we do that

contributes to our salvation. This was to counter what he saw to be Pelagius's too confident and optimistic understanding of the capacities of the human person, apart from God's grace, and his denial of original sin.

When later pressed by Julian of Eclanum to show where this "original sin'" was to be found, Augustine pointed to concupiscence, which is both an effect of original sin and leads to sin. Concupiscence itself is the disordered desire or appetite. When a person gives consent of the will to concupiscence, this is sin. For Augustine, the act of sexual intercourse after the Fall, even within marriage, is tainted by concupiscence, even if it is not sinful on the part of the couple. And in this sense, every child born was affected by original sin. This was why it was necessary for the child to be reborn in baptism.

These positions of Augustine certainly had an influence on subsequent Christian theology. But, especially when they are read through the lens of the sixteenth-century controversies over justification, there can be a tendency to isolate these positions from the rest of his thought or from the rest of the tradition. Augustine himself never retracted his earlier writings against the Manicheans, with which I deal in this chapter. In fact, he reiterated them in the controversy with Julian (see, for example, "Answer to Julian," in *Answer to Pelagians II*, John E. Rotelle, ed., Roland J. Teske, trans., *The Works of Saint Augustine*, Part I, Vol. 24 [Hyde Park, NY: New City Press, 1998], pp. 293–99). And even in his controversy with Julian, he still maintained that the body was good, marriage was good, and children were good. For Augustine, sin was the cause of evil in the world. Moral evil (sin) was located principally in the disordered will. In other writings, he has a much broader view of concupiscence, associating it primarily with the lust for wealth or power and domination over others.

With regard to the question of the influence of Augustine's positions on original sin and concupiscence on the vast majority of the people of the Middle Ages, this is something that can only be shown by careful and painstaking scholarship. The following factors would need to be taken into account: his interpretation of the way original sin is passed on through concupiscence was never affirmed by any synod, council, or other teaching authority of the church. The church formally rejected some of the positions he developed in the heat of the Pelagian controversy pertaining to predestination and freedom of the will (see "The Synod of Arles, c. 473" and "The Council of Orange, 529" in *Documents of the Christian Church*, Henry Bettenson, ed. [Oxford, UK: Oxford University Press, 1999], pp. 65–66). Other theologians, most notably Thomas Aquinas, provided an account of original sin that was more positive about human nature, even after original sin, than Augustine's own account.

My own starting point in this book is the bodily, cultural practices of the Christian religion that pertain to lay people, and games and sports in particular. My task is to explain how it is that a religious culture could have emerged that incorporated the body to the extent that medieval Christianity did. For these purposes, the aspects of Augustine's thought that came to the fore in the controversy with the Manicheans, that are found in writers who preceded him and who came after him, as well as in the formal teaching of the church, lay the foundation for a clear explanation of the matter.

42. *Pseudo-Dionysus: The Complete Works*, Colm Luibheid, trans., preface by Rene Roques, intros. by Jaroslav Pelikan, Jean LeClerq, and Karlfried Froehlich, The Classics of Western Spirituality (New York: Paulist Press, 1987), p. 95. Because Dionysus was thought to be the Areopagite whose conversion is recorded in Acts, his writings had a more profound influence on medieval theology both in the West and in the East than they might have had otherwise. See *ODCC*, s.v. "Dionysus (6) the Pseudo-Areopagite."

43. Ibid., p. 91.

44. For both Augustine and Pseudo-Dionysus, the existence of the demons who do not have a body illustrates that evil is not dependent on bodily existence. As Pseudo-Dionysus wrote, "It is also obvious that the body is not the cause of evil in the soul. Evil does not require a body to be nearby, as is clear in the case of demons. Evil in minds, in souls, and in bodies is a weakness and a

defect in the condition of their natural virtues" (*Pseudo-Dionysus: The Complete Works*, p. 92).

45. Thomas Aquinas, *Summa Contra Gentiles, Book 3: Providence*, Part I, trans. with intro. and notes, Vernon J. Bourke (Notre Dame, IN: University of Notre Dame Press, 1975), p. 50. The teaching of theologians like Augustine and Thomas Aquinas that God created all things, spiritual and corporeal, and that all things were good became the formal teaching of the church and expressed at church councils. The bishops at the Second Lateran Council (1215) taught over against the Albigensians and Cathars that the one true God in three persons is

> the one principle of the universe, the creator of all things, visible and invisible, spiritual and corporeal, who by His almighty power from the beginning of time made at once out of nothing both orders of creatures, the spiritual and the corporeal, that is, the angelic and the earthly, and then the human creature, who as it were shares in both orders, being composed of spirit and body. For the devil and the other demons were indeed created by God naturally good, but they became evil by their own doing. (*The Christian Faith*, p. 14)

The General Council of Florence in 1442 contained an affirmation of the goodness of all created things and a condemnation of Manichean views on the question of evil:

> (The Holy Roman Church) most firmly believes, professes and proclaims that the one true God, Father, Son, and Holy spirit, is the creator of all things, visible and invisible, who, when He so willed, out of His bounty made all creatures, spiritual as well as corporeal. They are good since they were made by Him who is the highest good, but they are mutable because they were made out of nothing. She asserts that there is no such thing as a nature of evil, because all nature, as nature, is good. Furthermore, the Church condemns the error of the Manicheans who asserted two first principles, one of visible, the other of invisible things,

and who said that the God of the New Testament is different from the God of the Old Testament. (*The Christian Faith*, p. 132)

46. See Thomas Aquinas, *Summa Theologica*, Vol. I, Pt. I, Q. 76, Fathers of the English Dominican Province, trans. (New York: Benziger Brothers, 1947). For most theologians and spiritual writers during the medieval period, the soul was thought to have three kinds of powers: vegetative, sensitive, and rational. As Hugh of St. Victor wrote, "One kind supplies life to the body alone in order that, on being born, the body may grow and, by being nourished, may remain in existence; another provides the judgment of sense perception; a third rests upon the power of mind and reason" (Hugh of St. Victor, *The Didascalicon of Hugh of St. Victor: A Medieval Guide to the Arts*, Jerome Taylor, trans. [New York: Columbia University Press, 1961], pp. 48–49). None of the three powers was thought to possess the capacities of the soul that pertained to the levels higher than their own. The function of the first power, for example, was to "attend to the forming, nourishing, and sustaining of bodies....It is the vivifying force seen at work in grasses and trees and whatever is rooted firmly in the earth" (Hugh of St. Victor, *The Didascalicon*, p. 49).

The higher powers of the soul included the capacities belonging to the powers below them, however. Animals, for example, who have sense perception, also have the first power of the soul, the vegetative, which nourishes their bodily existence and allows them to stay alive. Human beings, who are unique in that they possess reason, the third power of the soul, also possess the first two powers, the vegetative and the sensitive. This meant that the human soul was present in the most intimate details of human physicality and experience. It was also the soul that connected human beings to all other living things.

Other writers stressed the fact that the soul was present in each and every part of the human body to make a similar point. As William of St. Thierry put it, "The soul is in its body somewhat as God is in the world. Everywhere and everywhere entire. It is entire in each sense, so that the entire soul senses in each; it is entire in each part, so that the entire soul gives vegetative and animal life to the whole body" (William of St. Thierry, "The Nature of the Body and the Soul," in *Three Treatises on Man: A Cistercian Anthropology*, Bernard McGinn, ed. [Kalamazoo, MI: Cistercian Publications, 1977], p. 141).

47. Brian Davies, *The Thought of Thomas Aquinas* (New York: Oxford University Press, 1993), p. 210.

48. Quoted in Davies, *The Thought of Thomas Aquinas*, 210. The quote is from Thomas's *Summa Theologica*, Vol. 1, Pt. 1, Q. 75, art. 4.

49. *Summa Theologiae: A Concise Translation*, ed. Timothy McDermott (Notre Dame, IN: Ave Maria Press, 1991), pp. 131–32. Thomas distinguishes his own theory of knowledge from Plato's: "But Plato, considering only the immateriality of the human intellect, and not its being united in any way to a body, held that the objects of the intellect are separate ideas" (Thomas Aquinas, *Summa Theologica*, Vol. 1, Pt. I, Q. 84, art. 7, 432).

50. Thomas Aquinas, *Summa Theologica*, Vol. 2, Pt. III, Q. 61, art 1.

51. John of Damascus, *On the Divine Images: Three Apologies against Those Who Attack the Divine Images* (Crestwood, NY: St. Vladimir's Seminary Press, 2000), pp. 60–61.

52. Ibid., p. 17.

53. Ibid., pp. 18–19.

54. Ibid., p. 75.

55. Ibid., pp. 23–24.

56. Ibid., p. 20. The appropriateness of the use of images in Christian worship was supported in several church councils. At the Second Council of Nicea in 787, the bishops taught, "For, the more frequently one contemplates these pictorial representations, the more gladly will he be led to remember the original subject whom they represent, the more too will he be drawn to it…" (*The Christian Faith*, p. 399). The bishops at the Fourth Council of Constantinople in 869–70 wrote that just as through the words contained in the holy Gospels all can reach salvation, "so, due to the action which these images exercise by their colours, all, wise

and simple alike, can derive profit from them. For, what speech conveys in words, pictures announce and bring out in colors" (*The Christian Faith*, p. 400).

57. John of Damascus, *On the Divine Images*, p. 37.

58. St. John Chrysostom, *Homilies on the Gospel of St. Matthew*, Philip Schaff, ed., *A Select Library of the Nicene and Post-Nicene Fathers*, Vol. X (Grand Rapids, MI: Eerdmans, 1975), p. 343.

59. *The Writings of Justin Martyr and Athenagoras*, Rev. Alexander Roberts and James Donaldson, eds. (Edinburgh: T.&T. Clark, 1879), p. 353. See "Extant Fragments of His Lost Work on the Resurrection."

60. St. Augustine, *Marriage and Virginity*, John E. Rotelle, ed., Ray Kearney, trans., *The Works of Saint Augustine*, Part I, Vol. 9 (Hyde Park, NY: New City Press, 1999), p. 203.

61. St. Augustine, *City of God*, p. 551.

62. Ibid., pp. 554–55.

63. Ibid., p. 555.

64. St. Augustine, *Marriage and Virginity*, p. 204.

65. Thomas Aquinas, *Summa Theologica*, Vol. 1, Pt. I–II, Q. 61, art. 2.

66. Etienne Gilson, *The Christian Philosophy of St. Thomas Aquinas* (Notre Dame, IND: University of Notre Dame Press, 1956), p. 286.

67. Ibid.

68. Thomas Aquinas, *Summa Theologica*, Vol. 1, Pt. I–II, Q. 62, art. 1.

# CHAPTER 4: "I HAVE RUN THE RACE, I HAVE FOUGHT THE FIGHT"

The chapter title is a quotation from 2 Timothy 4:7.

1. It is significant that the writers of the New Testament and the theologians of the early Christian church made use of the Septuagint (Greek) version of the Old Testament. This Greek

translation was regarded by the Church fathers until the end of the fourth century as the standard version of the Old Testament. And the whole of the New Testament was written in Greek. Christianity was intimately related to Greek language and culture, then, from the beginning.

2. Roman Garrison, "Paul's Use of the Athlete Metaphor," *Studies in Religion* 22, no. 2 (1993): 211. Originally, the prize for first place at the Isthmian games was a wreath made of pine leaves. But the prize was changed in the fifth century to a wreath made of wild celery, in imitation of the Nemean games. One or the other of these plants was used as the first-place prize in games after this time. See Panos Valvanis, *Games and Sanctuaries in Ancient Greece: Olympia, Delphi, Isthmia, Nemea, Athens* (Los Angeles: Getty Museum, 2004), p. 281. According to Garrison, the custom of awarding the winners with nothing more than a wreath of leaves was an example of the purity of ancient Greek athletics. For Dan Dombrowski, however, the reality of the Panhellenic games was more complex than this interpretation suggests. He points out, for example, that the winner of Panhellenic games, like the Isthmian games, would receive a free meal every day for the rest of his life and many other such "perks" (Daniel Dombrowski, *Contemporary Athletics and Ancient Greek Ideals* [Chicago: University of Chicago Press, 2009]), p. 21.

3. Garrison quotes Epictetus, who wrote:

It is difficulties that show what men are. Consequently, when a difficulty befalls, remember that God, like a physical trainer, has matched you with a rugged young man. "For what purpose?" someone will say. So that you may become an Olympic victor, but that cannot be done without sweat.

The man who exercises himself against outward appearances is the true athlete in training....Great is the struggle, divine the task. The prize is a kingdom, freedom, serenity, peace. Remember God. Call upon him to help you and to stand by your side.

God says to you, "Give me proof that you have striven by the rules, eaten what is prescribed, taken exercise, heeded your trainer."

Now God says to you, "Come at last to the contest (*ton agona*) and show us what you have learned and how you have trained yourself. How long will you exercise alone? Now the time has come for you to discover whether you are one of the athletes who deserve victory or belong to the number of those who travel about the world and are everywhere defeated." (Epictetus, *Discourses* 1.24.1–2; II.18.27–29; III.10.8; IV.4.30. Quoted in Garrison, "Paul's Use of the Athlete Metaphor," *Studies in Religion* 22, no. 2 (1993): 210)

4. Garrison refers to the following Pauline texts as examples of how he understands self-control in relation to the ability to adapt to different circumstances: Philippians 4:11–13, 1 Timothy 6:6, Galatians 5:22–23, and Romans 8:35–37. He also points out that there is a striking parallel between the writings of Paul and the teachings of the Stoics with respect to these themes. For example, Epictetus wrote:

Who then is the invincible man? He whom nothing that is outside the sphere of his moral purpose can dismay. I consider the circumstances one by one, as I would do in the case of the athlete.

This fellow has won the first round. What, then, will he do in the second? What if it be scorching hot? And what will he do at Olympia?

It is the same way in the present case. If you put silver in a man's way, he will despise it. Yes, but what about a beautiful woman, or darkness or the hope of glory? What about abuse or praise? Or death, what then? All these things can be overcome....The man who passes all these tests is what I mean by the invincible athlete (Epictetus, *Discourses* I.18.21–23. Quoted in Garrison, "Paul's Use of the Athlete Metaphor," 212).

5. St. Clement of Rome, in a late first-century letter to the church at Corinth, which was experiencing problems with jeal-

ousy and envy, reviewed the way jealousy and envy wreaked havoc in the experiences of the Israelite people. Then he wrote, "Let us come to the athletes nearest to us in time. Let us take the noble examples of our own generation" (Clement of Rome, "The Epistle to the Corinthians," in *The Epistles of St. Clement of Rome and St. Ignatius of Antioch*, James A. Kleist, SJ, trans., Ancient Christian Writers: The Works of the Fathers in Translation [Westminster, MD: Newman Press, 1961], p. 12). By the "athletes nearest to us in time" he means "the good Apostles: Peter, who through unmerited jealousy underwent not one or two, but many hardships and, after thus giving testimony, departed for the place of glory that was his due" (p. 12). And Paul, who "through jealousy and strife...demonstrated how to win the prize of patient endurance: seven times he was imprisoned; he was forced to leave and stoned; he preached in the East and the West; and, finally, he won the splendid renown which his faith had earned" (p. 12).

6. Quoted in Garrison, p. 214. This sermon enjoyed considerable influence in the early church and later, in part because it was wrongly attributed to St. Clement.

7. Ambrose, "Letters," in *Library of the Fathers* (Oxford, 1881), Vol. 45, Ep. xliii, 4–6.

8. Recall Allen Guttmann's comment cited in chapter 3:

The mortal bodies mangled in the arena were, of course, less prized by the faithful than were the immortal souls they housed. In fact, "house" is too weak a metaphor to express the asceticism that was unquestionably a part of Christian piety. References to the human body as a prison, a charnel house, a grave, or a sink of corruption were ubiquitous in the religious literature of late antiquity and the Middle Ages as ascetic men and women were inspired to join the ranks of "those who made themselves eunuchs for the kingdom of Heaven" (Matthew 19:2)." (Allen Guttmann, *The Erotic in Sports*, p. 35)

9. Ignatius of Antioch, "To Polycarp," in *The Epistles of St. Clement of Rome and St. Ignatius of Antioch*, p. 96.

10. Ibid., p. 97.

11. Eusebius, *The Ecclesiastical History*, Roy J. Deferrari, trans., The Fathers of the Church (New York: Fathers of the Church, 1953), p. 272.

12. Ibid., p. 277.

13. Ibid., 282.

14. Ibid., p. 282. In the Gospel of Matthew, Jesus had encouraged his followers to recognize him as present in those who were experiencing physical suffering or who were marginalized and excluded. "For I was hungry and you gave me food, I was thirsty and you gave me something to drink, I was a stranger and you welcomed me, I was naked and you gave me clothing, I was sick and you took care of me, I was in prison and you visited me....Just as you did it to one of the least of these who are members of my family, you did it to me" (Matt 25: 35–36; 40).

15. Ibid., pp. 282–83.

16. Ibid., pp. 286–87.

17. Ibid., p. 287.

18. St. John of Damascus, *On the Divine Images: Three Apologies against Those Who Attack the Divine Images*, David Anderson, trans. (Crestwood, NY: St. Vladimir's Seminary Press, 2000). St. John cites this passage of Basil's on pp. 35–36.

19. John Cassian, *The Institutes*, Dennis McManus, ed., Boniface Ramsey, OP, trans., Ancient Christian Writers (New York: Newman Press, 2000), p. 123. The scripture quotation is from 2 Timothy 2:5.

20. Ibid., p. 124.

21. Ibid.

22. Ibid. This quote is taken from the chapter of the *Institutes* on "Gluttony." For Cassian, "This is our first contest, then; this is, as it were, our first trial in the Olympic Games—the extinguishing of the belly's desire to gormandize out of a yearning for perfection" (Cassian, *Institutes*, p. 125).

23. Ibid., pp. 272–73.

24. He writes:

Do you want to listen to the true athlete of Christ as he engages by lawful right in the combat? "I do not run," he says, "in uncertainty. I do not fight as one beating against the air. But I chastise my body and subject it to servitude, lest when preaching to others I be rejected myself." You see that he has found the most important aspect of the struggle in himself—that is, in his own flesh—and that he considers this to be an absolutely fundamental principle; and you see that he has linked the outcome of the fight solely to the chastisement of his flesh and the subjection of his body. And so, "I do not run in uncertainty." He does not run in uncertainty because, in looking upon the heavenly Jerusalem, he is clear as to where his swift and undeviating heart should be directed. He does not run in uncertainty because, "forgetting what is behind," he stretches himself out "to what is before," pressing "on to the goal, to the prize of the heavenly calling of God in Christ Jesus." Ever directing his mind's gaze to this and hastening to it with utter alacrity of heart, he cried out confidently: "I have fought the good fight, I have won the race, I have kept the faith." (Cassian, *Institutes*, p. 127)

25. Ibid., p. 127.

26. John Cassian, *The Conferences*, Walter J. Burghardt, John Dillon, Dennis D. McManus, eds., Boniface Ramsey, OP, trans. Ancient Christian Writers (New York: Paulist Press, 1997), p. 730.

27. Ibid.

28. Ibid., p. 732.

29. John Chrysostom, "An Address on Vainglory and the Right Way for Parents to Bring Up Their Children," M.L.W. Laistner, ed. and trans., *Christianity and Pagan Culture in the Later Roman Empire: Together with an English Translation of John Chrysostom's "An Address on Vainglory and the Right Way for Parents to Bring up Their Children"* (Ithaca, NY: Cornell University Press, 1967), p. 112.

30. Ibid., p. 95.

31. Ibid., pp. 113–14.

32. Ibid., p. 122. John Sawhill's research demonstrates the remarkable extent to which John Chrysostom made use of athletic metaphors in his biblical homilies. See John Alexander Sawhill, *The Use of Athletic Metaphors in the Biblical Homilies of St. John Chrysostom* (Princeton, NJ: Princeton University Press, 1928).

33. *The Didascalicon of Hugh of St. Victor: A Medieval Guide to the Arts*, Jerome Taylor, trans. (New York: Columbia University Press, 1961).

34. For Hugh, philosophy is the "discipline which investigates comprehensively the ideas of all things, human and divine" (Hugh of St. Victor, *The Didascalicon*, p. 51).

35. Hugh divides philosophy into four categories, "the theoretical, which strives for contemplation of truth; the practical, which considers the regulation of morals; the mechanical, which supervises the occupations of this life; and the logical, which provides the knowledge necessary for correct speaking and clear argumentation" (Hugh of St. Victor, *The Didascalicon*, p. 60).

36. Ibid., p. 79.

37. Ibid.

38. Jerome Taylor writes that a crude index of the influence of *The Didascalicon* on its own and later ages is that it was found in nearly one hundred different manuscripts of the twelfth through the fifteenth centuries, preserved in some forty-five libraries throughout Europe from Ireland to Italy, Poland to Portugal (Hugh of St. Victor, *The Didascalicon*, p. 4).

39. Thomas Aquinas, *Summa Theologica*, Vol. 2, Pt. II–II, Q. 168, art. 2. Fathers of the English Dominican Province, trans. (New York: Benziger Brothers,. 1947).

40. Ibid.

41. Ibid.

42. Ibid., Pt. II–II, Q. 168, art. 3. In another place, Thomas writes that one should be careful when at play not to "lose the balance of one's mind altogether" (Thomas Aquinas, *Summa Theologica*, Pt. II–II, Q. 168, art. 2). He quotes Ambrose: "'We should beware lest, when we seek relaxation of mind, we destroy all that harmony which is the concord of good works' (*De Offic.* I.

20),'" and Cicero, who wrote, "'Just as we do not allow children to enjoy absolute freedom in their games, but only that which is consistent with good behavior, so our very fun should reflect something of an upright mind' (*De Offic.* I)" (Thomas Aquinas, *Summa Theologica*, Pt. II–II, Q. 168, art. 2).

43. Ibid.

44. Ibid., Pt. II–II, Q. 168, art. 4.

45. Ibid., Pt. II–II, Q. 168, art. 3.

46. Ibid.

47. *Albert and Thomas: Selected Writings*, Simon Tugwell, trans. and ed. (Mahwah, NJ: Paulist Press, 1988), pp. 527–28.

48. Ibid., p. 527.

49. Ibid.

50. Cardinal Nicholas Cusanus, *The Game of Spheres*, Pauline Moffit Watts, trans. (New York: Abaris Books, 1986), p. 55.

51. Ibid., p. 57.

52. Ibid., p. 69.

53. Ibid., p. 71.

54. Ibid.

55. Ibid. Nicholas's doctrine of the soul was more influenced by Plato than many of the approaches we considered in chapter 3. It was not uncommon for the humanists to be influenced by Plato, given that they had enthusiastically retrieved the classical sources for reflection. Plato's influence is evident in that Nicholas at times writes about the soul having better access to the truth the further it is removed from the body. But he still holds that the human person is a unity of body and soul. For him, the soul exists simultaneously in every part of the body; and sensuality, imagination, reason, and intellect are "diverse modes of apprehending in the soul" (Cusanus, *The Game of Spheres*, p. 67).

56. Ibid., p. 77.

# CHAPTER 5: "ORDINARY PEOPLE, JUST FRANKLY ENJOYING THEMSELVES LIKE HUMAN BEINGS"

The chapter title is a quotation from Harold Frederic, *The Damnation of Theron Ware.*

    1. Catholic priests were not allowed by law in New England or in New York after the English took it over from the Dutch in 1664. An act passed in New York in 1700 read that any Jesuit, priest, or missionary who preaches or teaches the Catholic faith or celebrates Mass or "other of the Romish Ceremonies & Rites of worship…shall be deemed and Accounted an incendiary and disturber of the publick peace and Safety and an Enemy to the true Christian Religion and shall be adjudged to Suffer perpetuall Imprisonm't and if any person being So Sentenced and actually Imprisoned shall break prison…he shall Suffer such paines of Death penalties and forfeitures as in Cases of felony" (Edwin S. Gaustad, ed., *A Documentary History of Religion in America: To the Civil War* [Grand Rapids, MI: Eerdmans, 1982], p. 147). The same act declared that anyone who harbored or succored a Jesuit, priest, or missionary would be fined.

> Whereas divers Jesuits priests and popish missionaries have of late come and for Sometime have had their residence in the remote parts of this Province…and by their wicked and Subtle Insinuations Labour to Debauch, Seduce and w'draw the Indians from their due obedience unto his most Sacred ma'ty and Stir them up to Sedition Rebellion and open Hostility against his ma'tys Goverm't.…It is hereby enacted… that all and every Jesuit and Seminary Priest missionary or other Spirituall or Ecclesiasticall person made or ordained by any Authority power or Jurisdicon derived Challenged or p'tended from the Pope or See of Rome now resideing w'th in this province or any part thereof shall depart from and out of the Same at or before the

first day of November. (Gaustad, *A Documentary History*, p. 147)

In 1641 the colony of Virginia decreed, "it shall not be lawful …for any popish priest that shall hereafter arrive here to remain above five days…" (Gaustad, *A Documentary History*, pp. 96–97).

It is curious that Catholics are typically overlooked in books about the history of recreation, sport, and leisure in America. Foster Rhea Dulles, in his book *A History of Recreation: American Learns to Play* (2d ed. [New York: Appleton-Century-Crofts, 1965]), for example, does not mention Catholics, even though they were the largest church (when compared with Protestant denominations taken singularly) in the United States already by the turn of the twentieth century. Dulles focuses all of his attention on Protestants, and the story there is a familiar one: the Puritans rejected virtually all forms of recreation; this was intensified again with the revivals in the middle of the nineteenth century; then more liberal forms of Protestantism began to be more accepting of this aspect of culture in the late nineteenth century, contributing to the acceptance of sport as an aspect of American culture. Cindy Aron's book, *Working at Play: A History of Vacations in the United States* (Oxford, UK: Oxford University Press, 1999), repeats much the same story line as Dulles's, emphasizing the way the Protestant work ethic has influenced leisure activities and vacations in the United States. She does not mention Catholics.

2. Joseph T. Durkin, *Georgetown University: First in the Nation's Capital* (Garden City, NY: Doubleday, 1964), p. 5.

3. "College of George-town, (Potomack) in the State of Maryland, United States of America, 1798," Washington, DC: Georgetown University, Lauinger Library, Georgetown University Archives [GUA].

4. "Georgetown College, In the District of Columbia, United States of America, under the Direction of the Incorporated Catholic Clergy of the State of Maryland," 1809, GUA.

5. "A.M.D.G. Georgetown College, District of Columbia, under the Direction of the Incorporated Catholic Clergy of Maryland," 1814, GUA.

# Notes

6. Durkin, *Georgetown University*, p. 12.

7. "Catalogue of the Officers and Students of St. Joseph's College, Bardstown, KY., 1857–1858," Detroit, MI: University of Detroit-Mercy Library, Archives of the Detroit Province of the Society of Jesus.

8. "Descriptive Catalogue, Santa Clara College, 1878–1879," Santa Clara, CA: Santa Clara University, Orradre Library, Santa Clara University Archives.

9. Ibid. This description would have been apt almost twenty years earlier in 1860, judging from an article written by "Professor Anderson," a traveler from England, which had been published in the *Sunday Atlas*. Before his visit to Santa Clara College, Anderson "could not see how the members of a church, the motto of whose banner is 'Semper Eadem,' could adapt themselves to the exigencies of the present age and educate their pupils in accordance with the requirements of the day in which we live. On both those points I received enlightenment, and was very agreeably surprised" (Professor Anderson, "A Reminiscence of California, Being a Visit to a Jesuit College," *Sunday Atlas*, Sunday, October 21, 1860). He writes:

> Most agreeable was it to see the arrangements made for the physical health of the pupil, that being rightly considered as essential to mental and moral sanity. I was shown a very large play ground and an excellent gymnasium adjacent. I found the study-room to be extensive and admirably well ventilated; and the sleeping apartments to be especially well arranged and scrupulously clean. They surpassed in every way the dormitories of Eton College and of Rugby School in England. Warm baths are provided for winter use, while for summer diversion, there is a bathing pond.... Should the student suffer from sickness, there is an infirmary for him to recuperate in. An apothecary's shop is attached to it, and a first class physician pays his visits daily." (Anderson, "A Reminiscence of California")

10. *Georgetown College Journal* V, no. 5 (February 1877), GUA. This essay is attributed to De Courcey, but the tone and quality of the writing suggest that he probably had some help writing it. The editor, more polemically minded than the author of the essay, couldn't help inserting the following observation: "The sects have done diametrically the opposite, and so, have made their converts either gloomy formalists or imperfectly varnished hypocrites. Ed."

11. Ibid.

12. "Directions for Novitiate," Los Gatos, CA: Archives of the California Province of the Society of Jesus.

13. *Georgetown College Journal* XXVI, no. 3 (December 1897), GUA.

14. "Prospectus of the St. Louis University, 1861–1862," Archives of the Detroit Province of the Society of Jesus.

15. *Georgetown College Journal* XIV, no. 2: 15, GUA.

16. *Georgetown College Journal* VII, no. 2: 15–16, GUA.

17. Christa Klein, "The Jesuits and Catholic Boyhood in Nineteenth Century New York City: A Study of St. John's College and the College of St. Francis Xavier, 1846–1912" (PhD diss., University of Pennsylvania, 1976), 255. She is quoting from "First Division Diary," *St. John's College*, August 2, 1904.

18. Ibid., pp. 254–55.

19. "Excursion of St. Joseph's Sodality," *Catholic Herald*, September 4, 1845. Philadelphia: Old St. Joseph's Parish, Parish Archives.

20. Ibid. For Paul, this excursion, which he describes as something of a feast for the senses, was a profoundly spiritual experience. He writes elsewhere in the letter, "There were 'rich viands,' the more substantial meats, peach, melon, pastry, ices, 'whatever the appetite could desire,' with sweet music 'the while,' breathing its witching cadence in the ear. The instrumental and vocal music, not to forget the sounds of nature, the warbling of birds, the chirping of insects, the sighing of the winds in the trees, and the rippling of the neighboring stream, all combined to ravish the senses and almost make one believe oneself transported from earth to fairy land" ("Excursion of St. Joseph's Sodality").

21. *The Adams-Jefferson Letters,* Lester J. Cappon, ed. (Chapel Hill: University of North Carolina Press, 1959), p. 474.

22. Ibid., p. 484.

23. Etolia S. Basso, ed., *The World from Jackson Square: A New Orleans Reader* (New York: Farrar, Straus, 1948), p. 139.

24. Ibid., p. 140.

25. Harold Frederic, *The Damnation of Theron Ware or Illumination* (New York: Stone & Kimball, 1896), p. 349.

26. Ibid., pp. 349–56.

27. David Maraniss, *When Pride Still Mattered: A Life of Vince Lombardi* (New York: Simon and Schuster, 1999), p. 20. That Vince Lombardi would play sports seemed as natural as that he would go to church. His father Harry had tattooed on the knuckles of his right and left hands the words WORK and PLAY, embodying an older European Catholic tradition that considered both activities as having a place in a virtuous life.

28. Ibid., p. 245. While Vince Lombardi's Catholic faith was of great importance to him and even influenced how he coached football (a topic Maraniss discusses insightfully), some influential approaches to the study of sport in the modern world tend to ignore the religious dimension of life. Allen Guttmann, for example, stresses the secular character of the modern world in which he understands modern sport to be situated. Lombardi's life was as far from the secular one that Guttmann describes as one can imagine, however. He tended to be a very traditional Catholic and was even hesitant about the changes in the church associated with Vatican II that opened the doors of the church to the modern world (see Allen Guttmann, *From Ritual to Record: The Nature of Modern Sports* [New York: Columbia University Press, 1978]).

Even when attempts are made to write about the religious dimension of sport in the United States, the Catholic faith of coaches, athletes, and others is sometimes written out of the picture. James Mathisen, for example, writes that Vince Lombardi and John F. Kennedy are the two people who best personified the emergence of sport as a "folk religion" in the United States, which he describes as a subset of the "religion of the American way of life." He only mentions in passing that Lombardi was an Italian Catholic immigrant and doesn't mention Kennedy's Catholic faith (which had been a very important issue for many Americans, especially non-Catholics, in a presidential election in 1960). (See James Mathisen, "From Civil Religion to Folk Religion: The Case of American Sport," in *Sport and Religion*, Shirl J. Hoffman, ed. [Champaign, IL: Human Kinetics Books, 1992]).

29. Maraniss, *When Pride Still Mattered*, p. 245. Maraniss comments:

> There has been a tendency in recent decades to mix sport and religion in the most superficial, public ways, with athletes proclaiming that God healed an injury or guided the winning shot, that a comeback victory was the Lord's work, as though the Father and the Son, if not the Holy Ghost, were taking sides and cared one whit about the outcome of games. It would be difficult to find someone who conjoined sport and religion more deeply than Lombardi, but as an old-line Catholic, trained by the Fordham Jesuits, he accomplished this in a more personal way, without proselytizing. (p. 243)

30. Ibid., pp. 408–9.

31. Julie Byrne, *O God of Players: The Story of the Immaculata Mighty Macs* (New York: Columbia University Press, 2003), p. 10.

32. Ibid., pp. 10–11.

33. Ibid., p. 7.

34. Ibid., p. 4.

35. Ibid., p. 5.

36. Ibid., pp. 23–24. Competition at these games was intense. One official of these games remembers, "You sometimes had an escort to get out of the gym as the official," she said. "Usually a nun. Nobody would mess with a nun" (Byrne, *O God of Players*, 24).

37. Ibid., p. 27.

38. Ibid., pp. 125–26.

39. Ibid., p. 127.

40. Ibid.

41. Ibid.

42. Ibid., p. 131. The 1948–1949 Immaculata Catalogue reads, "Knowledge and learning must be integrated with life....The *whole* student must be educated." Students would learn in the classroom, but also "through their experiences in chapel,...library, laboratories, residence halls, and on the athletic field" (Byrne, *O God of Players*, p. 131).

43. Julie Byrne, "'O God of Players': Immaculata College Basketball and American Catholic Women's Pleasure, 1939–1975" (PhD diss., Duke University, 2000), p. 294.

44. Byrne, *O God of Players*, p. 130.

# CHAPTER 6: "A FORM OF GYMNASTICS OF THE BODY AND OF THE SPIRIT"

The chapter title is a quotation from Pope John Paul II, "Pope to Milan Football Team."

1. John Paul II, "Pope to Milan Football Team," *L'Osservatore Romano* (May 28, 1979): 4.

2. John Paul II, "During the Time of the Jubilee: The Face and Soul of Sport," October 28, 2000 (Rome: Holy See), http://www.vatican.va/holy_father/john_paul_ii/speeches/documents/hf_jp.

3. John Paul II, "The Most Authentic Dimension of Sport," *L'Osservatore Romano* (April 24, 1984): 3.

4. Ibid.

5. John XXIII, "The Educational Value of Sports," in *The Lay Apostolate*, Monks of Solesmes, eds. (Boston: St. Paul Editions, 1961), p. 584.

6. Paul VI, "Values in Sports Competitions," *L'Osservatore Romano* (May 22, 1975): 8.

7. Unpublished message of Pope Benedict XVI to Cardinal Stanislaw Rylko, president of the Pontifical Council for the Laity on the occasion of the international study seminar on "Sport,

Education, Faith: Toward a new Season for the Catholic Sports Movement."

8.   Richard Baxter, *A Christian Directory or a summ of practical theologie and cases of conscience* (London: Printed for Richard Edwards, 1825), p. 619.

9.   Quoted in William Hogan, "Sin and Sport," in *Motivations in Play, Games and Sports*, Ralph Slovenko and James Knight, eds. (Springfield, IL: Charles C. Thomas, 1967), pp. 124–25.

10.   Bill Pennington, "As Team Sports Conflict, Some Parents Rebel," *New York Times*, November 12, 2003, sec. A, p. 1 and sec. C, p. 16.

11.   Ibid.

12.   Bill Pennington, "Doctors See a Big Rise in Overuse Injuries for Young Athletes," *New York Times*, February 22, 2005, http://www.nytimes.com.

13.   Ibid.

14.   Phil Jackson and Hugh Delehanty, *Sacred Hoops: Spiritual Lessons of a Hardwood Warrior* (New York: Hyperion, 1995), p. 90.

15.   David L. Fleming, SJ, *Draw Me into Your Friendship, The Spiritual Exercises: A Literal Translation and Contemporary Reading* (St. Louis: Institute of Jesuit Sources, 1996), p. 113. This quotation is taken from Fleming's contemporary reading of the literal text of Ignatius's *Exercises*. For Ignatius, it is *characteristic* for people to be led astray in the spiritual life in this way. But this is not the only way for this to happen, in his view.

16.   Pier Paolo Vergerio, "The Character and Studies Befitting a Free-Born Youth," *Humanist Educational Treatises*, Craig W. Kallendorf, ed., The I Tattie Renaissance Library (Cambridge, MA: Harvard University Press, 2002), p. 77.

17.   Francois Pierron, *Le Bon Precepteur ou La belle maniere de bien elever la jeunesse pour Dieu, & pour le beau monde* (Lyon: Chez Horace Boissat & G. Remers, 1661), p. 223.

18.   Ibid., p. 221.

19.   "Floyd Landis," *New York Times*, May 10, 2010. See http://topics.nytimes.com/top/reference/timestopics/people/l/floyd_landis/index.html.

20. Lynn Zinzer, "USC Sports Receive Harsh Penalties," *New York Times*, June 10, 2010, http://www.nytimes.com. I am bracketing the larger question about whether all of the NCAA rules regarding the operation of intercollegiate athletics make sense.

21. Romano Guardini, *The Spirit of the Liturgy* (New York: Crossroad, 1997), p. 70.

22. Ibid., pp. 71–72.

23. Peter Berger, *A Rumor of Angels: Modern Society and the Rediscovery of the Supernatural* (Garden City, NY: Anchor Books, Doubleday & Co., 1970), p. 60.

24. Edward Everett Hale, *Public Amusement for Poor and Rich* (Boston: Phillips, Sampson and Co., 1857), p. 21.

25. Washington Gladden, *Amusements: Their Uses and Abuses* (North Adams, MA: James T. Robinson & Co, 1866), p. 6.

26. Horace Bushnell, *Christian Nurture* (Charles Scribner: New York, 1861), pp. 339–40.

27. Ibid.

28. Harvey Cox, *The Feast of Fools: A Theological Essay on Festivity and Fantasy* (Cambridge, MA: Harvard University Press, 1969), p. 146.

29. Ibid., p. 13.

30. Johan Huizinga, *Homo Ludens: A Study of the Play Element in Culture* (Boston, MA: Beacon Press, 1968).

31. Randolph Feezell, *Sport, Play and Ethical Reflection* (Champaign: University of Illinois Press, 2006).

32. Ibid., pp. 25–26.

33. See Mihaly Csikszentmihalyi, *Beyond Boredom and Anxiety: The Experience of Play in Work and Games* (San Francisco: Jossey Bass, 1975). For theological reflection on the flow experience in sport, see Patrick Kelly, SJ, "Flow, Sport and the Spiritual Life," chap. 7 in *Theology, Ethics and Transcendence in Sport*, Jim Parry, Nick Watson, and Mark Nesti, eds. (New York: Routledge, 2010).

34. St. Augustine, "Answer to an Enemy of the Law and the Prophets," in *Arianism and Other Heresies*, John E. Rotelle, ed. intro., trans. and notes, Roland J. Teske, SJ, *Works of Saint Augustine:*

*A Translation for the 21st Century,* Part I, Vol. 18 (New York: New City Press, 1995), pp. 360–61.

35. Jackson and Delehanty, *Sacred Hoops,* p. 79.

36. Ibid.

37. Geet Sethi with Sunil Agarwal, *Success vs. Joy* (New Delhi, India: 20:20 Media, 2004), pp. 223–24.

38. Ibid., p. 224.

39. Ibid., p. 225.

40. Ibid., p. 63.

41. Klaus Meier, "An Affair of Flutes: An Appreciation of Play," *Journal of the Philosophy of Sport* VII (1980): 27. The quote within the quote is from Josef Pieper, *Leisure, the Basis of Culture* (New York: Random House, 1963), 4.

42. Adapted from the entrance prayer at the Mass prior to the changes introduced at the Second Vatican Council. At these liturgies, after the sign of the cross, the priest would say (in Latin): "I will go unto the altar of God." And the people would respond, "To God, who gives joy to my youth."